The Merrill Studies
in
Billy Budd

CHARLES E. MERRILL STUDIES

Under the General Editorship of
Matthew J. Bruccoli and Joseph Katz

The Merrill Studies
in
Billy Budd

Compiled by

Haskell S. Springer
University of Kansas

Charles E. Merrill Publishing Company
A Bell & Howell Company
Columbus, Ohio

Standard Book Number: 675-09364-3

Library of Congress Catalog Number: 71-112875

1 2 3 4 5 6 7 8 9 10 — 79 78 77 76 75 74 73 72 71 70

Printed in the United States of America

Preface

The selections in this volume are necessarily only a small sampling of the hundreds of articles and chapters of books which, since 1921, have attempted to cope with the intricacies of Herman Melville's last long fictional work. However, these pieces, chosen for their historical importance, representative viewpoints, or creative insights, cumulatively ask the most meaningful questions and venture many of the more reasonable and exciting answers about *Billy Budd*. But to understand this collection fully, and to be able to comprehend some otherwise cryptic references in these readings, one should first know some pertinent facts about Melville, about the composition and history of *Billy Budd* itself, and about the trends in *Billy Budd* criticism.

In 1886, at the age of 67, Melville retired from his position as a deputy inspector of customs in New York City, and at about the same time began work on a narrative which eventually became *Billy Budd*.[1] Melville's period of great productivity had ended almost thirty years before, with *The Confidence Man*, and *Moby-Dick* was thirty-five years in the past; yet now, in the last few years of his life he wrote again with the depth and breadth of perception that distinguishes his best work. This morally profound and complex novel has intrigued generations of critics, who, unfortunately, have written under unusual handicaps to interpretation. For, as Melville worked on his story, his concept of it changed, and

---

[1] See Harrison Hayford and Merton M. Sealts, Jr., eds., *Billy Budd, Sailor (An Inside Narrative)* (Chicago, 1962), p. 2.

87977

he revised often enough so that at his death in 1891 his manuscript was not yet in final form, ready for the printer. In fact, some of his pages were left in near chaos. Consequently, the subsequent history of the novel has consisted of repeated scholarly attempts to decipher Melville's notations and fathom his final intentions.[2] Knowledge of these editorial efforts is vitally important to the student of *Billy Budd* because an article written in 1930 interprets a somewhat different text than one composed in 1950, which in turn criticizes a different *Billy Budd* than a critique written in 1965.

Billy Budd appeared in print for the first time in 1924, edited by Raymond Weaver, who, four years later, published a modified version of his edition. Unfortunately, though both were far from accurate, almost all *Billy Budd* criticism for twenty years depended on these two printings. In 1948 H. Barron Freeman, after a scholarly reexamination of the manuscript, produced an edition which came much closer to what Melville had actually intended. But Freeman too made many errors in transcription and interpretation, some of which, we can see now, obviously misled critics who depended on his text. Freeman was in error, as was Weaver, in thinking that Melville intended to title his narrative *Billy Budd, Foretopman,* and that the author meant *"Indomitable"* to be the name of Captain Vere's ship. More important, like Weaver, Freeman mistakenly printed what he considered to be the author's "Preface" to *Billy Budd.* In this piece, Melville speaks of the French Revolution in connection with the mutinies in the British Navy at Spithead and the Nore, saying that like the revolution in France, the Great Mutiny ultimately brought about much-needed reforms. Freeman, in addition, thought he detected in Melville's manuscript an early state of the novel, which he called a "short story" and printed as a separate part of his edition.

Most recently, in 1962, Harrison Hayford and Merton M. Sealts, Jr. published their impressive *Billy Budd, Sailor (An Inside Narrative),* including both a reading text, and a "genetic text" which shows in detail the many stages in Melville's five-year reworking of his material. Using the greatest care in manuscript analysis and transcription, they demonstrate, with supporting evidence and convincing argument, that their title was Melville's final choice for his novel. They show too that *"Bellipotent,"* not *"Indomitable,"* was the intended name of the British man-of-war, and that Mel-

---

[2]For a detailed account of the novel's textual history, see Hayford and Sealts, pp. 12-24.

ville's supposed "Preface" was actually a cancelled portion of a late chapter. They argue, furthermore, that no short story or proto-*Billy Budd* as Freeman had printed it ever existed.

These textual matters are clearly reflected in *Billy Budd* criticism. In this volume, for example, Norman Holmes Pearson's eclectic article refers to Melville's supposed "early draft" as identified by Freeman, and H. Bruce Franklin's mythic study finds that although the mere change of a name might seem a small matter, Melville's final choice of *"Bellipotent"* is meaningful to the story in ways *"Indomitable"* could never be. The supposed "Introduction" to the novel is mentioned in several articles written before 1962, and other critics not represented in these pages have in all innocence made that spurious note the basis for their readings of the story.

But even ignoring the textual problems, scholars have found more than enough grist for their mills in other aspects of *Billy Budd*. A survey of the spectrum of *Billy Budd* criticism reveals that Melville's rich story has supported extremely diverse interpretations; among them are those based on the novel's mythic suggestiveness. Billy's sacrificial death, his record as a "peacemaker," and his comments on his parentage strongly imply a Christ-parallel which is reinforced by minor details and intensified by his "ascension" at his execution. His radical innocence, in addition, links him with Adam before the Fall. Classical and biblical allusions add to his heroic and mythic stature, as does his attack on the embodiment of evil. Critics have also found other, less familiar, mythic and religious suggestions in Billy — and rather obvious ones in Claggart, who, with his snake-like characteristics and antipathy toward good, is clearly satanic.

Although Captain Vere, unlike the two other major figures in the tale, has not been the subject of mythic interpretation, he has served as the focus of much thoughtful criticism. A number of commentators, perceiving that Melville's picture of Vere is drawn in more detail than even Billy's, have treated him and not the Handsome Sailor as the moral center of the book. In the eyes of many, Vere's unusual strength of character, his distinct philosophical superiority to most naval men, and his full understanding of the "moral phenomenon" presented by Billy Budd, are drastically qualified if not negated by his insistence that the hastily-convened court condemn Billy to immediate death. But harsh and time-serving as it may seem, say opposing critics, Vere's course of action, under the circumstances, is at least thoroughly justifiable: if Billy himself accepts the justice of the punishment and calls down God's blessing on Vere, should we balk? Yes! is the response of those uncomfortable with the idea of a noble Captain Vere; Billy knows not what he does.

Source-hunters too have found *Billy Budd* tantalizing because of its intriguing historical and literary references. For example, in the course of the story, Melville explicitly compares Vere, ironically or not, with Lord Nelson, and also comments on the Great Mutiny. Such details have led scholars to search the historical record and Melville's reading, where they have found that the often-referred-to *Somers* case — in which Melville's cousin Guert Gansevoort sat on the shipboard court which condemned several sailors to death — is only one of several incidents in naval history and lore, British and American, which may well have influenced Melville's thinking. Others, looking for parallels in literature in their search for possible inspiration or even direct sources for *Billy Budd,* have made convincing arguments for resemblances to popular literature of the time as well as for the apparent influence of some major works such as *Paradise Lost* and *The Winter's Tale.* Comparisons with other great works of ages past also occur in some of the criticism which addresses the question of the form or genre of *Billy Budd.* Is Melville's novel a tragedy? If not, how far short does it fall? Here the fact of an unfinished manuscript complicates once again the job of the critic.

The best recent criticism pays careful attention to the incompleteness of *Billy Budd,* and is cautious about advancing final, all-embracing judgments. But a more complete understanding of the work's difficulties and shortcomings has not apparently lessened the desire for full comprehension of its meaning. Consequently, like the critics of the 1920's, those of the 1960's must still attack the vexing problem of Melville's tone. A few have been led to say that an unfinished work cannot have a finished tone, and to attribute to incompleteness the great critical disagreements on ultimate meaning; but most seem to have taken to heart Melville's assertion in Chapter Twenty-eight of *Billy Budd* that "truth uncompromisingly told will always have its ragged edges," and continue to take sides in the ongoing discussion of the personal attitudes Melville embodies in his story.

Although the earlier critics, like those today, were divided on the question of whether Melville narrates *Billy Budd* in his own voice or uses a persona, the 1920's, 30's and 40's showed few major disagreements about the work's tone. Articles frequently pointed out that *Billy Budd* was the product of an old man, and often added that it was a chastened, softened Melville who at the end of his life, after years of literary silence, had spoken out in terms of serenity and even hope. Gone was the fiery, rebellious Melville who had created that "grand, ungodly, god-like man," Captain Ahab. Most agreed that a life of questioning and bitter disillusionment had ended with an "everlasting yea," an acceptance, however sad, of the way of the world. Whether an expression of hope or merely a recognition of necessity, *Billy Budd* still had an essential calmness. But in 1950 Joseph Schiffman questioned that "God bless Captain Vere" was an affirmative statement for Melville. "As innocent Billy utters these words," Schiffman asked, "does not the reader gag?" This approach to *Billy Budd* as an ironic document was expanded by a number of critics who generally felt that though Melville had used a subdued style in *Billy Budd*, the man behind the words was unsubdued yet, was still shaking his fist at the universe.

Since 1962, of course, the critic has had a trustworthy text, and has been quite precise and exacting in analyzing intention or tone. Some of Hayford and Sealts' suggestions of "perspectives for criticism" have been taken up, and their genetic text has supported several excellent close readings which try to avoid the acceptance-irony polarization formerly dominant. The establishment of a text actually turns out to have increased interpretive possibilities rather than restricted them; and ultimately all these critical efforts impose no limits on meaning in *Billy Budd*, but rather suggest that a fine work of imagination will renew itself with each reader, or at least with each generation. It is, then, with both the great achievement and the further potential of *Billy Budd* criticism in mind that the reader should approach this collection. The last word has not been spoken.

Note

The chronologically arranged selections in this volume are reprinted from their original places of publication, without change in text, though I have corrected many misquotations and other errors, and changed footnote numbers where necessary.[3] Where

---

[3]Mr. Sutton has made some stylistic changes in his essay, and Mr. Bowen has added a long footnote to explain an important disagreement with Hayford and Sealts.

an article before 1962 refers to the text only by chapter number,
I have emended its references to accord with the Hayford-Sealts
numbering. The reader will find, too, that at times the quotations
from *Billy Budd* in pre-1962 criticism vary slightly from the now-
standard text. In no case, however, is a selection in this volume
based on an earlier textual reading now contradicted by the
Hayford-Sealts version. Likewise, though several pieces herein
mention Melville's supposed "Preface," I have excluded all interpretations which depend primarily on it for their support.

HSS

Contents

The Merrill Studies
in
Billy Budd

John Middleton Murry

From "Herman Melville's Silence"

. . . And the thirty-five years of silence began. At the extreme end of them, moved perhaps by a premonition of coming death, Melville wrote another "story." "Billy Budd" is carefully dated: it was begun on November 16, 1888, the rewriting began on March 2, 1889, and it was finished on April 19, 1891. In the following September Melville was dead. With the mere fact of the long silence in our minds we could not help regarding "Billy Budd" as the last will and spiritual testament of a man of genius. We could not help expecting this, if we have any imaginative understanding. Of course, if we are content to dismiss in our minds, if not in our words, the man of genius as mad, there is no need to trouble. Some one is sure to have told us that "Billy Budd," like "Pierre," is a tissue of naivety and extravagance: that will be enough. And, truly, "Billy Budd" *is* like "Pierre" — startlingly like. Once more Melville is telling the story of the inevitable and utter disaster of the good and trying to convey to us that this must be so and ought to be so — chronometrically and horologically. He is trying, as it were with his

From *Times Literary Supplement,* No. 1173 (July 10, 1924), p. 433. Reprinted by permission of Times Newspapers, Ltd.

1

final breath, to reveal the knowledge that has been haunting him —
that these things must be so and not otherwise.

Billy Budd is a foretopman, pressed out of the merchant service
into the King's Navy in the year of the Nore mutiny. He is completely good, not with the sickly goodness of self-conscious morality, but as one born into earthly paradise — strong, young, manly,
loyal, brave, unsuspecting, admired by his officers and adored by
his shipmates. And he is hated by the master-at-arms, the police-
man of the lower deck. Claggart hates him, simply because he is
Billy Budd, with the instinctive hatred of the evil for the good.
Melville is careful to explain that there is no reason whatever for
his hatred; he puts it deliberately before us as naked and elemental — the clash of absolutes. Claggart is subtle and cool, he works
quietly, and he is also a man of courage. He involves Billy Budd
in the thin semblance of revolutionary mutiny. The master-at-
arms deliberately risks his own life in order to destroy his enemy's.
He risks it, and loses it, for in the privacy of his own cabin the
captain confronts the accuser with his victim, and in a flash of
anger Budd strikes the master-at-arms dead. This moment in the
story is unearthly. But Billy Budd is doomed: he has killed his
officer in time of war. The captain who understands and loves him
presides over the court-martial, and Budd is condemned to be
hanged at dawn.

.   .   .

That is the story, told with a strange combination of naïve and
majestic serenity — the revelation of a mystery. It was Melville's
final word, worthy of him, indisputably a passing beyond the nihil-
ism of "Moby Dick" to what may seem to some simple and child-
ish, but will be to others wonderful and divine.

John Freeman

From *Herman Melville*

If it seems fantastic to compare *Moby-Dick* with Milton's *Paradise Lost* and assert a parallel conception in each, it will seem fantastic to say that in a shorter story, *Billy Budd*, may be found another *Paradise Regained*.

Like *Moby-Dick* this late and pure survival of Melville's genius has a double interest, the interest of story and the interest of psychology. *Billy Budd* is the narrative of one who, like Pierre, is unpractised in the ways of life and the hearts of other men; guilelessness is a kind of genius and the better part of innocence in this handsome young sailor.

. . .

Exaltation of spirit redeems such a scene [as the hanging] from burdens which otherwise might appear too painful to be borne. And beyond this, it is innocence that is vindicated, more conspicuously in death than it could be in life. Melville's MS. contains a

From *Herman Melville* (New York: The Macmillan Co., 1926), pp. 131, 135-136. Reprinted by permission of the publishers.

3

note in his own hand — "A story not unwarranted by what happens in this incongruous world of ours — innocence and infirmity, spiritual depravity and fair respite"; the ultimate opposition is shown clearly here in this public vindication of the law, and the superior assertion at the very moment of death of the nobility of a pure human spirit. *Moby-Dick* ends in darkness and desolation, for the challenge of Ahab's pride is rebuked by the physical power and the inhumanness of Nature; but *Billy Budd* ends in a brightness of escape, such as the apostle saw when he exclaimed, "O death, where is thy sting?"

Finished but a few months before the author's death and only lately published, *Billy Budd* shows the imaginative faculty still secure and powerful, after nearly forty years' supineness, and the not less striking security of Melville's inward peace. After what storms and secret spiritual turbulence we do not know, except by hints which it is easy to exaggerate, in his last days he re-enters an Eden-like sweetness and serenity, "with calm of mind, all passion spent", and sets his brief, appealing tragedy for witness that evil is defeat and natural goodness invincible in the affections of man. In this, the simplest of stories, told with but little of the old digressive vexatiousness, and based upon recorded incidents, Herman Melville uttered his everlasting yea, and died before a soul had been allowed to hear him.

E. M. Forster

From *Aspects of the Novel*

Billy Budd is a remote unearthly episode, but it is a song not without words, and should be read both for its own beauty and as an introduction to more difficult works. Evil is labelled and personified instead of slipping over the ocean and round the world, and Melville's mind can be observed more easily. What one notices in him is that his apprehensions are free from personal worry, so that we become bigger not smaller after sharing them. He has not got that tiresome little receptacle, a conscience, which is often such a nuisance in serious writers and so contracts their effects — the conscience of Hawthorne or of Mark Rutherford. Melville — after the initial roughness of his realism — reaches straight back into the universal, to a blackness and sadness so transcending our own that they are undistinguishable from glory.

From *Aspects of the Novel* (New York: Harcourt, Brace & World, Inc., 1927), p. 206. Reprinted by permission of the publishers.

5

Raymond Weaver

From *Shorter Novels of Herman Melville*

Just as some theologians have presented the fall of man as evidence of the great glory of God, in similar manner Melville studies the evil in Claggart in vindication of the innocence in Billy Budd. For, primarily, Melville wrote *Billy Budd* in witness to his ultimate faith that evil is defeat and natural goodness invincible in the affections of man. *Billy Budd*, as *Pierre*, ends in disaster and death; in each case inexperience and innocence and seraphic impulse are wrecked against the malign forces of darkness that seem to preside over external human destiny. In *Pierre, Melville* had hurled himself into a fury of vituperation against the world; with *Billy Budd* he would justify the ways of God to man. Among the many parallels of contrast between these two books, each is a tragedy (as was Melville's life), but in opposed senses of the term. For tragedy may be viewed not as being essentially the representation of human misery, but rather as the representation of human goodness or nobility. All of the supremest art is tragic: but the tragedy is, in Aristotle's phrase, "the representation of Eudaimonia," or

From the Introduction to *Shorter Novels of Herman Melville* by Herman Melville (New York, 1928), pp. 1-li. Permission of Liveright, Publishers, New York. Copyright © 1956 by Liveright Publishing Corporation.

the highest kind of happiness. There is, of course, in this type of tragedy, with its essential quality of encouragement and triumph, no flinching of any horror of tragic life, no shirking of the truth by a feeble idealism, none of the compromises of the so-called "happy ending." The powers of evil and horror must be granted their fullest scope; it is only thus we can triumph over them. Even though in the end the tragic hero finds no friends among the living or dead, no help in God, only a deluge of calamity everywhere, yet in the very intensity of his affliction he may reveal the splendor undiscoverable in any gentler fate. Here he has reached, not the bottom, but the crowning peak of fortune — something which neither suffering nor misfortune can touch. Only when worldly disaster has worked its utmost can we realize that there remains something in man's soul which is forever beyond the grasp of the accidents of existence, with power in its own right to make life beautiful. Only through tragedy of this type could Melville affirm his everlasting yea. The final great revelation—or great illusion—of his life, he uttered in *Billy Budd*.

Carl Van Doren

From "A Note of Confession"

... Billy Budd surpasses the best of Conrad in the music of its language, as in the profundity and serenity of its reflections.

Billy Budd is particularly important among the works of Melville because in it alone he rises above the dark problems which tormented the later years of his life. No longer asking himself, of course vainly, why evil should exist, he asks instead how it moves on its horrid errands and what is to be done about it. Or rather, he answers by telling the story of Billy Budd, a handsome sailor who is hated by a petty officer on the ship, is unjustly accused to the captain, in a burst of worthy indignation strikes the petty officer and unintentionally kills him, and has to be hanged for his offense though the captain believes the sailor to be essentially without guilt. Hardly anywhere in fiction is there a more penetrating representation of native malice than in Melville's account of how Claggart comes to hate Billy for his beauty and his innocence. The processes of Iago are superficial in comparison. Seldom in fiction has any character been so powerfully and lucidly exhibited in any such moral plight as that of Captain Vere, faced with

From *The Nation,* CXXVII (December 5, 1928), 622.

a plain duty and a conscience plainly urging him not to do it. And neither of these parts of the story is so memorable as the scene, at once terrible and exalted, in which Billy, innocent of everything but innocence and manslaughter, is hanged, the victim of his own victim, who was evil as Billy was innocent. The innumerable implications of the plot are broodingly revealed. Wisdom surrounds it as the water surrounds the ship. But the narrative has none of the dispersion, as of light in a prism, which often goes with wisdom. In this last story Melville wrote he thought of all he had ever thought, and yet moved forward through it with the tense, straight line of art.

Lewis Mumford

From *Herman Melville*

... Billy Budd, his final novel, is not a full-bodied story: there is statement, commentary, illustration, just statement, wise commentary, apt illustration: what is lacking is an independent and living creation. The epithets themselves lack body and colour: Billy Budd has nothing to compare with the description of boiling whaleoil in Moby-Dick — "a wild Hindoo odour, like the left wing of the Day of Judgement."

Billy Budd, which was dedicated to Jack Chase, wherever he might be, alow or aloft, lacks the fecundity and energy of White-Jacket: the story itself takes place on the sea, but the sea itself is missing, and even the principal characters are not primarily men: they are actors and symbols. The story gains something by this concentration, perhaps: it is stripped for action, and even Melville's deliberate digressions do not halt it. Each of the characters has a Platonic clarity of form.

. . .

From *Herman Melville* (New York: Harcourt, Brace & World, Inc., 1929), pp. 353-354, 356-357. Reprinted by permission of the publishers.

10

Billy Budd is the story of three men in the British Navy: it is also the story of the world, the spirit, and the devil. Melville left a note, crossed out in the original manuscript, "Here ends a story not unwarranted by what happens in this incongruous world of ours — innocence and infirmity, spiritual depravity and fair respite." The meaning is so obvious that one shrinks from underlining it. Good and evil exist in the nature of things, each forever itself, each doomed to war with the other. In the working out of human institutions, evil has a place as well as the good: Vere is contemptuous of Claggart, but cannot do without him: he loves Budd as a son and must condemn him to the noose: justice dictates an act abhorrent to his nature, and only his inner magnanimity keeps it from being revolting. These are the fundamental ambiguities of life: so long as evil exists, the agents that intercept it will also be evil, whilst we accept the world's conditions: those universal articles of war on which our civilizations rest. Rascality may be punished; but beauty and innocence will suffer in that process far more. There is no comfort, in this perpetual Calvary, to find a thief nailed on either side of the Cross. Melville had been harried by these paradoxes in Pierre. At last he was reconciled. He accepted the situation as a tragic necessity; and to meet that tragedy bravely was to find peace, the ultimate peace of resignation, even in an incongruous world. As Melville's own end approached, he cried out with Billy Budd: God bless Captain Vere! In this final affirmation Herman Melville died. September 28, 1891, was the date of the outward event.

E. L. Grant Watson

"Melville's Testament of Acceptance"

Melville finished the short novel, *Billy Budd,* five months before his death in 1891. It was not published until 1924, when it was included in the Constable edition of 750 copies. No other printing has yet appeared.*

The style of this product of Melville's last years is strikingly different from the exuberant and highly-colored prose of that great period of more ardent creation (1850 to 1852) which produced *Mardi, Moby-Dick,* and *Pierre.* Though it lacks that fine extravagance of the earlier books, which laid on the color with prodigality, *Billy Budd* is as rich, or even richer, in Melville's peculiar and elaborate symbolism; and this symbolism becomes all the more effective for being presented in a dry and objective manner. The fine flourishes, the purple patches, which scintillate brilliantly in *Moby-Dick,* and the deep sombre melancholy of *Pierre* are not here. The grandiloquence of youth which tempted Stevenson's very partial appreciation is here transformed into the dignity of an achieved

From *The New England Quarterly,* VI (June 1933), 319-327. Reprinted by permission of *The New England Quarterly.*
*[Actually, Liveright had printed *Billy Budd* five years earlier, in 1928.— EDITOR.]

detachment. The story develops simply, always unhurried, yet never lagging. Each character is described with the patience which the complex intention of the theme demands — the color of the eyes, the clothes, the complexion, the color of the skin, of the blood under the skin, the past, the present — these are hints at a deep and solemn purpose, one no less ambitious than to portray those ambiguities of good and evil as the mutually dependant opposites, between which the world of realization finds its being.

The title *Billy Budd* is not without significance, and would strike some readers in its crude simplicity as proof that Melville was lacking in a sense of humor. How could any man, they would argue, write a tragedy and call it *Billy Budd*? But a sense of humor, like almost everything else, is relative. Melville certainly lacked it in the crude form; but he was always conscious of those occasions when he might seem, to a superficial view, to be wanting it. He is particularly conscious of the obvious, but not in the obvious manner; and when he uses such a name as *Billy Budd* to set as the hub round which his own philosophy of life must revolve, he does so consciously, choosing the obvious to carry the transcendental. "I have ever found the plain things, the knottiest of all," he has written; and so he has made the simple man, the every-day Billy, the handsome sailor, the hero of a tragedy. Humor is appreciated most easily when larger things contract suddenly to smaller things — as when a man slips on a piece of orange-peel, thus converting his intention of going about his business to the abrupt act of falling on his back-side. Yet a more imaginative intelligence might, with a sense of humor just as true, see in this fall, the destiny of man, with full chorus of pities and ironic spirits. The easy contraction will seem to the sophisticated too facile to provoke a smile, a larger humor is found in the reverse process, namely in a filling in, in an exaggeration from the particular to the general. With such an added pinch of imagination, the obvious thing becomes the centre of mystery. And so, with a sense of humor which perceived both the obvious and the peculiar quality of the name, Melville deliberately chose "Billy Budd." Moreover, he made the hero of this, his gospel story (as it might well be called), a foundling of uncertain parentage, whose "entire family was practically invested in himself."

It is a mistake for critics to try to tell stories which authors must have told better in their texts. The critic's function is rather to hint at what lies beneath — hidden, sometimes, under the surface. Melville called his story "an inside narrative," and though it deals with events stirring and exciting enough in themselves, it is yet more exciting because it deals with the relation of those principles which constitute life itself. A simple-mindedness unaffected by the shadow of doubt, a divine innocence and courage, which might suggest a Christ not yet conscious of His divinity, and a malice which has lost itself in the unconscious depths of mania — the very mystery of iniquity — these opposites here meet, and find their destiny. But Melville's theme is even larger. All the grim setting of the world is in the battleship *Indomitable;* war and threatened mutiny are the conditions of her existence. Injustice and inhumanity are implicit, yet Captain Vere, her commander, is the man who obeys the law, and yet understands the truth of the spirit. It is significant of Melville's development since the writing of *Moby-Dick* and *Pierre,* that he should create this naval captain — wholly pledged to the unnaturalness of the law, but sufficiently touched, at the same time, by the divine difference from ordinary sanity (he goes by the nick-name of "Starry Vere"), as to live the truth *within* the law, and yet, in the cruel process of that very obedience, to redeem an innocent man from the bitterness of death imposed by the same law. A very different ending this from the despairing acts of dissolution which mark the conclusions of the three earlier books: *Mardi, Moby-Dick,* and *Pierre.*

Melville is no longer a rebel. It should be noted that Billy Budd has not, even under the severest provocation, any element of rebellion in him; he is too free a soul to need a quality which is a virtue only in slaves. His nature spontaneously accepts whatever may befall. When impressed from the merchant-ship, the *Rights of Man,* he makes no demur to the visiting lieutenant's order to get ready his things for trans-shipment. The crew of the merchant-ship are surprised and reproachful at his uncomplaining acquiescence. Once aboard the battleship, the young sailor begins to look around for the advantages of chance and adventure. Such simple power to accept gives him the buoyancy to override troubles and irritations which would check inferior natures.

Yet his complete unconsciousness of the attraction, and consequent repulsion, that his youthful beauty and unsophisticated good-fellowship exercise on Claggart, make it only easier for these qualities to turn envy into hatred. His very virtue makes him the target for the shaft of evil, and his quality of acceptance provokes to action its complementary opposite, the sense of frustration that can not bear the consciousness of itself, and so has to find escape in mania. Thus there develops the conflict between unconscious virtue (not even aware of its loss of Eden and unsuspecting of the presence of evil) and the bitter perversion of love which finds its only solace in destruction.

And not only Billy Budd is marked by this supreme quality of acceptance. Captain Vere, also, possesses it, but with full consciousness, and weighted with the responsibility of understanding the natural naturalness of man's volition and the unnatural naturalness of the law. In the summing up at the drum-head court-martial of the case for the law against the innocent man, he said:

> How can we adjudge to summary and shameful death a fellow-creature innocent before God, and whom we feel to be so? — Does that state it right? You sign sad assent. Well, I too feel the full force of that. It is Nature. But do these buttons that we wear attest that our allegiance is to Nature? No, to the King. Though the ocean, which is inviolate Nature primeval, though this be the element where we move and have our being as sailors, yet as the King's officers lies our duty in a sphere correspondingly natural? . . . We fight at command. If our judgements approve the war, that is but coincidence. So in other particulars. So now, would it be not so much ourselves that would condemn as it would be martial law operating through us? For that law and the rigour of it, we are not responsible. Our vowed responsibility is in this: That however pitilessly that law may operate, we nevertheless adhere to it and administer it.

In Captain Vere we find a figure which may interestingly be compared to Pontius Pilate. Like Pilate, he condemns the just man to a shameful death, knowing him to be innocent, but, unlike Pilate, he does not wash his hands, but manfully assumes the full responsibility, and in such a way as to take the half, if not more than the half, of the bitterness of the execution upon himself. We are given to suppose that there is an affinity, a spiritual understanding between Captain Vere and Billy Budd, and it is even suggested that in their partial and separate existences they contribute two essential portions of that larger spirit which is man. Such passages as that quoted lie on the surface of this story, but they indicate the depths beneath. There are darker hints: those deep, far-away things in Vere, those occasional flashings-forth of intuition—short, quick probings to the very axis of reality. Though the book be read many times, the student may still remain baffled by Melville's significant arrangement of images. The story is so solidly filled out as to suggest dimensions in all directions. As soon as the mind fastens upon one subject, others flash into being.

Melville reported in *Pierre* how he fished his line into the deep sea of childhood, and there, as surely as any modern psychoanalyst, discovered all the major complexes that have since received baptism at the hands of Freudians. He peered as deep as any into the origins of sensuality, and in conscious understanding he was the equal of any modern psychologist; in poetic divination he has the advantage of most. No doubt the stresses of his own inner life demanded this exceptional awareness. In this book of his old age, the images which he chose for the presentation of his final wisdom, move between the antinomies of love and hate, of innocence and malice. From behind — from far behind the main pageant of the story — there seem to fall suggestive shadows of primal, sexual simplicities. In so conscious a symbolist as Melville, it would be surprising if there should be no meaning or half-meaning in the spilling of Billy's soup towards the homosexually-disposed Claggart, in the impotence of Billy's speech in the presence of his accuser, in his swift and deadly answer, or the likening of Claggart's limp, dead body to that of a snake.

It is possible that such incidents might be taken as indications of some unresolved problem in the writer himself. This may be, but when we remember how far Melville had got in the process of self-analysis in *Pierre,* and when we have glanced at the further analysis that is obvious in the long narrative poem *Clarel,* it seems likely that this final book, written nearly forty years after *Pierre,* should contain a further, deeper wisdom. And as the philosophy in it has grown from that of rebellion to that of acceptance, as the symbolic figures of unconscious forces have become always more concrete and objective, so we may assume that these hints are intentional, and that Melville was particularly conscious of what he was doing.

But let no one suppose that he would ever pin an image to his scale of value, as an entomologist would pin an insect to his board; there is always in his interpretation a wide spaciousness. He lifts some familiar object, holding it to his light, that it may glow and illumine some portion of what must always remain vast and unknown. For his suggestive use of words, and the special values he gives them, and the large implication he can in this way compress into a sentence, the passage which tells how Billy Budd was hanged from the main yard-arm of the battle-ship *Indomitable* is a good example:

Billy stood facing aft. At the penultimate moment, his words, his only ones, words wholly unobstructed in the utterance, were these—

"God bless Captain Vere!" Syllables so unanticipated coming from one with the ignominious hemp about his neck — a conventional felon's benediction directed aft towards the quarters of honour; syllables, too, delivered in the clear melody of a singing bird on the point of launching from the twig, had a phenomenal effect, not unenhanced by the rare personal beauty of the young sailor, spiritualised now through late experiences so poignantly profound.

Without volition, as it were, as if indeed the ship's populace were the vehicles of some vocal current-electric, with one voice, from alow and aloft, came a resonate echo — "God bless Captain Vere!" And yet at that instant Billy alone must have been in their hearts, even as he was in their eyes.

At the pronounced words and the spontaneous echo that voluminously rebounded them, Captain Vere, either through stoic self-control or a sort of momentary paralysis induced by emotional shock, stood erectly rigid as a musket in the ship-armourer's rack.

The hull, deliberately recovering from the periodic roll to leeward, was just regaining an even keel, when the last signal, the preconcerted dumb one, was given. At the same moment it chanced that the vapoury fleece hanging low in the east, was shot through with a soft glory as of the fleece of the Lamb of God seen in mystical vision, and simultaneously therewith, watched by the wedged mass of upturned faces, Billy ascended; and ascending, took the full rose of the dawn.

In the pinioned figure, arrived at the yard-end, to the wonder of all, no motion was apparent save that created by the slow roll of the hull, in moderate weather so majestic in a great ship heavy-cannoned.

Here is Melville at his very best, at his deepest, most poetic, and therefore at his most concentrated, most conscious. Every image has its significant implication: the very roll of the heavily-cannoned ship so majestic in moderate weather — the musket in the ship-armourer's rack; and Billy's last words are the triumphant seal of his acceptance, and they are more than that, for in this supreme passage a communion between personality at its purest, most-God-given form, and character, hard-hammered from the imperfect material of life on the battleship *Indomitable*, is here suggested, and one feels that the souls of Captain Vere and Billy are at that moment strangely one.

In this short history of the impressment and hanging of a handsome sailor-boy, are to be discovered problems almost as profound as those which puzzle us in the pages of the Gospels. *Billy Budd* is a book to be read many times, for at each reading it will light up, as do the greater experiences of life, a beyond leading always into the unknown.

F. O. Matthiessen

From *American Renaissance*

... In one of his *Battle-Pieces* [Melville] had already expressed the conclusion that

> No utter surprise can come to him
> Who reaches Shakespeare's core;
> That which we seek and shun is there—
> Man's final lore.

In creating *Lear* or *Macbeth* Shakespeare did not seek good and shun evil. He sought and shunned one and the same thing, the double-faced image of life. It is hardly too much to say that Melville's quatrain is one of the most comprehending perceptions ever made of the essence of tragedy.

Throughout *Billy Budd* Melville gave testimony that he had grown into possession of what he had perceived in those lines. He showed too what he had meant by calling his age shallow. He knew, as he had known in *The Confidence Man*, that something more than mere worldly shrewdness was necessary for understand-

From F. O. Matthiessen, *American Renaissance* (New York, 1941), pp. 512-514. Copyright 1941 by Oxford University Press, Inc. Reprinted by permission.

ing such characters as those of his villain and hero. We have observed how often in his final story he reinforced himself at critical instances by Biblical allusions. His concern with both Testaments, pervasive throughout his work, now gave rise to his laconic statement that the great masters of legal policy, Coke and Blackstone, 'hardly shed so much light into obscure spiritual places as the Hebrew prophets.' Melville believed that he could probe Claggart's depravity only by means of the illumination gained in meditating on the Scriptural phrase, 'mysteries of iniquity.' And only by profound acceptance of the Gospels was he able to make his warmest affirmation of good through a common sailor's act of holy forgiveness.

At the time of Captain Vere's announcement of Billy's sentence, Melville remarked that it 'was listened to by the throng of standing sailors in a dumbness like that of a seated congregation of believers in Hell listening to their clergyman's announcement of his Calvinistic text.' At that point Melville added in the margin of his manuscript the name of Jonathan Edwards. The rectitude of Vere seems to have recalled to him the inexorable logic, the tremendous force of mind in the greatest of our theologians. Melville might also have reflected that the relentless denial of the claims of ordinary nature on which Edwards based his reasoned declaration of the absolute Sovereignty of God had left its mark on the New England character, on such emotionally starved and one-sided figures as Hawthorne drew, on the nightmare of will which a perverted determinism had become in Ahab. Without minimizing the justice of Vere's stern mind, Melville could feel that the deepest need for rapaciously individualistic America was a radical affirmation of the heart. He knew that his conception of the young sailor's 'essential innocence' was in accord with no orthodoxy; but he found it 'an irruption of heretic thought hard to suppress.'[1] The hardness was increased by his having also learned what Keats had, through his kindred apprehension of the meaning of Shakespeare, that the Heart is the Mind's Bible. Such knowledge was the source of the passionate humanity in Melville's own creation of tragedy.

How important it was to reaffirm the heart in the America in which *Billy Budd* was shaped can be corroborated by the search

---

[1] Freeman's edition places this significant comment in its proper context for the first time. Weaver's inaccurate placing of it made it refer to the way that Christianity is distorted by a chaplain's lending its sanction to a man-of-war. [The Hayford-Sealts edition omits the phrase entirely.—EDITOR.]

that was being made for the drift of significance in our eighteen-eighties and nineties by two of our most symptomatic minds. John Jay Chapman was already protesting against the conservative legalistic dryness that characterized our educated class, as fatal to real vitality; while Henry Adams, in assessing his heritage, knew that it tended too much towards the analytic mind, that it lacked juices. Those juices could spring only from the 'depth of tenderness,' the 'boundless sympathy' to which Adams responded in the symbol of the Virgin, but which Melville — for the phrases are his — had found in great tragedy. After all he had suffered Melville could endure to the end in the belief that though good goes to defeat and death, its radiance can redeem life. His career did not fall into what has been too often assumed to be the pattern for the lives of our artists: brilliant beginnings without staying power, truncated and broken by our hostile environment. Melville's endurance is a challenge for a later America.

Frederic Barron Freeman

From *Melville's* Billy Budd

The story and novel of Billy Budd are tragedies in prose fiction and should, therefore, effect a satisfying emotional purge in the reader. The characters and situations are valid; the prose is rhythmic and moving; and the issues raised by the story are significant to perceptive men. The hero, although he is not strong-willed and defiant like Ahab, comes to the same tragic end and meets it with strength and courage. But, since he has never resisted, never "reasoningly" tried to save himself or that for which he stands, the story might seem to end with a deadening sense of futility and hopelessness in the face of evil unpurged. It is in the final scenes, in the description of Billy's death and what followed, that the catharsis is effected. A tragedy cannot end happily. Also, to be a great tragedy, it cannot end without the purge and tranquillity which come through greater understanding and leave a note of hope. The evil characters may go unpunished; but if, through the death of the hero, their sin is realized and understood

Reprinted by permission of the publishers from *Melville's* Billy Budd, as edited by Frederic Barron Freeman and corrected by Elizabeth Treeman (Cambridge, Mass.: Harvard University Press, 1948), pp. 125-126. Copyright 1948, 1956 by the President and Fellows of Harvard College.

by some of the participants in the tragedy, then a catharsis is achieved and the spectator or reader is made to feel that, however dark the future looks, through this new-found comprehension at least some good can come from evil. Thus, after the rising calm of Billy's death-scene which has lent a positive, upward surge to the reader's emotions, the truth of his sacrifice is spread abroad, not through those who wrote the blindly intellectual "official report" of the case, but through the common, illiterate sailors who made a legend of the event.

The calm description of Billy's ascension could not have been accidental on Melville's part. A comparison of it with the paragraphs in *Moby Dick* which describe the sinking of the *Pequod* reveals both how calculated the imagery and tone of the two passages are and how contrasting are the two works' final verdicts on the nature of the force that rules the universe. Tragic nobility and defeat are the keynotes of the closing pages of *Moby Dick;* hope and triumph in death form the final ascendant notes of Billy's tragedy. Certain parallels between the characters of the two tales make the contrasting tones of their final pages more vivid. Ishmael, the understanding observer, like Captain Vere, the knowing arbiter, saw and felt the full truth. Both Moby Dick and Claggart were only agents of evil. But when the crashing sea surges over the masts of the *Pequod* and drags down the bird of heaven with its archangelic shrieks, the reader experiences a calculated effect which is in direct contrast to Billy's ascension into the calm sky of the rising sun, with "no motion apparent save that created by the ship's motion, in moderate weather so majestic in a great ship ponderously cannoned." Here, as in *Moby Dick*, the sacrifice is made, the evil realized — but here it is realized in a calm, ascending note of hope.

Joseph Schiffman

"Melville's Final Stage, Irony: A Re-examination of *Billy Budd* Criticism"

The aged Melville, like the Dansker of *Billy Budd,* "never inter-feres in aught and never gives advice." Melville wrote *Billy Budd,* his last work, without interjecting moral pronouncements; for this reason the story is usually taken as Melville's "Testament of acceptance," or, in the latest and most extended criticism, as Melville's "Recognition of necessity." Most critics, by mistaking form for content, have missed the main importance of *Billy Budd.* Actually, Melville's latest tale shows no radical change in his thought. Change lies in his style. *Billy Budd* is a tale of irony, penned by a writer who preferred allegory and satire to straight narrative, and who, late in life, turned to irony for his final attack upon evil.[1]

From *American Literature,* XXII (May 1950), 128-136. Reprinted by permis-sion of Duke University Press and the author.

[1] The present writer owes his thanks to Professor Gay Wilson Allen for first suggesting that *Billy Budd* might best be understood as a work of irony.

F. Barron Freeman, in his long critical introduction to his own edition of *Billy Budd,* comes close to recognizing the vital role of irony in the tale when he observes: "outward events become submerged in inward delineations and sometimes make the impatient reader wish for more definite statements, more tangible proof, that what the personages and the tale seem to imply is what Melville intended." See F. Barron Freeman, *Melville's Billy Budd* (Cam-bridge, Mass., 1948), p. 51. Freeman gives a good deal of evidence of irony in *Billy Budd,* but he twists it into conformity with "the Christian doctrine of resignation." His interpretation will be discussed later in this paper. Quota-tions from *Billy Budd* are from the Freeman text.

23

Billy Budd is a simple, naïve sailor removed from the merchant
ship *Rights-of-Man* and impressed into service in His Majesty's
Navy to fight the French revolutionists in the year 1797. Aboard
H.M.S. *Indomitable*, he unhappily finds himself the object of un-
reasoning hatred by John Claggart, Master-at-Arms of the ship.
Claggart denounces Billy to Captain Vere as a mutineer. Vere,
aware that the charge is groundless, offers Billy the opportunity to
face Claggart and make effective reply. But Billy, who stutters in
moments of stress, cannot summon his speech organs to his defense. Exasperated in his inability to refute the lie, Billy strikes
Claggart, who falls dead. Captain Vere, contemptuous of the dead
body of Claggart, exclaims, "Struck dead by an angel of God. Yet
the angel must hang!" For this is a time of revolutions, and the
English Navy has been racked with rebellion; an empire may be
lost. Discipline must be maintained. "Forms, measured forms" are
all. And so, Billy Budd, morally innocent, must die for striking
and killing a petty officer of His Majesty's Navy. Billy, before
going to his death, shouts aft, "God bless Captain Vere," honoring the author of his fate.

Billy's last words, "God bless Captain Vere," have been taken
by almost all critics to be Melville's last words, words of accommo-
dation, resignation, his last whispered "acceptance" of the realities
of life. Mumford, for example, says: "At last he [Melville] was
reconciled . . . [he found] the ultimate peace of resignation. . . . As
Melville's own end approached, he cried out with Billy Budd:
God bless Captain Vere!"[2]

The disillusioned of the world toasted Melville as a long-
unclaimed member of their heartbroken family. Here indeed was a
prize recruit—Melville, the rebel who had questioned "the inalien-
able right to property, the dogmas of democracy, the righteousness
of imperialist wars and Christian missions . . . [who] dared to discuss in a voice louder than a whisper such horrific subjects as
cannibalism, venereal disease and polygamy . . ."[3] had, in the ripe
wisdom of old age, uttered "God bless Captain Vere," thereby
accepting authority. A prize catch indeed, if it were really so!

E. L. Grant Watson tips his hat to the Melville of *Billy Budd:*

> Melville [he says] is no longer a rebel. It should be noted that
> Billy Budd has not, even under the severest provocation, any ele-
> ment of rebellion in him; he is too free a soul [this man with the

---

[2] Lewis Mumford, *Herman Melville* (New York, 1929), p. 357.
[3] From Willard Thorp's Introduction to *Herman Melville, Representative
Selections* (New York, 1938), p. xcvii.

rope around his neck] *to need a quality which is a virtue only in slaves.* . . . Billy Budd is marked by this *supreme quality* of acceptance. . . . [Melville's] philosophy in it has *grown* from that of rebellion to . . . acceptance. . . .[4]

Watson's bias towards a philosophy of acceptance is clear; he searches in Melville for confirmation of his own dogma.

Charles Weir, Jr., makes much of the "God bless Captain Vere" scene, accepting it at face value. He says: "The paradox has been established: injustice [the hanging of Billy] may find its place within the pattern of a larger all-embracing divine righteousness."[5] What this all-embracing divine righteousness may be is not specified. Is Vere God? Or is he, as he himself very clearly sets forth, the agent of the King? If the latter, then Billy is the unhappy pawn in a game he never understood, aristocratic England versus democratic France.

Both Watson and Weir warn the reader that Melville must be plumbed and probed if he is to surrender his secrets. Watson says, "The critic's function is rather to hint at what lies beneath — hidden, sometimes, under the surface."[6] Weir warns that, "in writing *Billy Budd* Melville had a deeper intent than that of simply telling a story."[7] And yet Watson and Weir ignore their own good advice, for in propounding their theory of Melville's "acceptance," they do not probe beneath Billy's last words. They accept "God bless Captain Vere" as the denouement of the tale, its final judgment, as the ripe wisdom of a tired Melville come to terms with life.[8]

These critics, it seems to me, commit three basic mistakes in their attempt at divining Melville's final moments of thought in his story. First, they divorce *Billy Budd* from all of Melville's other works in the way that a man might search for roots in treetops. Second, they isolate Melville from the Gilded Age, the time in which Melville produced *Billy Budd*.[9] Third, and most important,

---

[4] E. L. Grant Watson, "Melville's Testament of Acceptance," *New England Quarterly*, VI, 319-327 (June, 1933) (italics mine).
[5] Charles Weir, Jr., "Malice Reconciled: A Note on Melville's Billy Budd," *University of Toronto Quarterly*, XIII, 276-285 (April, 1944).
[6] Watson, *op. cit.*, p. 321.
[7] Weir, *op. cit.*, p. 280.
[8] The fullest treatment of the theory of Melville's "acceptance" can be found in William Ellery Sedgwick, *Herman Melville: The Tragedy of Mind* (Cambridge, Mass., 1945), pp. 231-249. Thorp agrees with Sedgwick. He says: "With good reason, *Billy Budd* has been called 'Melville's testament of acceptance . . .'" (*Literary History of the United States*, New York, 1948, I, 469).

they accept at face value the words "God bless Captain Vere," forgetting that Melville is always something other than obvious. It is the purpose of this paper to examine Melville's final work along the lines suggested.

Little is known of Melville's last days, and this should be recognized as a handicap for those who wish to prove the theory of Melville's "acceptance" as well as for those who may hold contrasting views. But the few scraps that do remain of Melville's later life point to an unchanged Melville, the same Melville of *Moby-Dick* and *Pierre*.[10] Mumford reports that in 1871 Melville studied Spinoza, marking a passage which read: " 'Happiness . . . consists in a man's being able to maintain his own being. . . .' " Mumford goes on to observe significantly: "[This] described [Melville's] own effort. In a more fruitful age, his being would have been maintained in harmony with, not in opposition to, the community; but at all events his vital duty was to maintain it."[11] This is an unchanged Melville. Another scrap of information, from a letter to a British fan, indicates Melville's critical frame of mind in 1885. To James Billson he wrote: "It must have occurred to you, as it has to me, that the further our civilization advances *upon its present lines*, so much the cheaper sort of thing does 'fame' become, especially of the literary sort."[12]

These lines, written just three years before he began *Billy Budd*, sound remarkably like the Melville who more than thirty years before had said of Pierre: "The brightest success, now seemed intolerable to him, since he so plainly saw, that the brightest success could not be the sole offspring of Merit; but of Merit for the one thousandth part, and nine hundred and ninety-nine combining and dovetailing accidents for the rest. . . ."[13]

Matthiessen, in discussing the aging Melville and his *Billy Budd*, significantly speaks of the effects of the Gilded Age on the thinking

---

[9] F. O. Matthiessen is the only critic to my knowledge who has attempted to place Melville in the context of the Gilded Age, that most disastrous of periods for the serious American writer. See Matthiessen, *American Renaissance* (New York, 1941), pp. 513-514.

[10] Freeman says of the aged Melville: "He was not embittered. He was polite, old, independent, and busy. He had not forgotten his works. He was still writing them" (*op. cit.*, p. 11).

[11] Mumford, *op. cit.*, p. 344. Despite this observation, Mumford, too, believes that Melville's post-Civil War days were "chastened" and "subdued" (p. 325).

[12] "Some Melville Letters," *Nation and Athenæum*, XXIX, 712-713 (Aug. 13, 1921) (italics mine).

[13] *Pierre* (New York, 1930), p. 377.

of American writers. He refers to John Jay Chapman's "protesting against the conservative legalistic dryness that characterized our educated class." and Henry Adams, who "knew that it [the educated class] tended too much towards the analytic mind, that it lacked juices."[14] Vere answers the description of an educated man characterized by legalistic dryness.

In almost all respects, *Billy Budd* is typically Melvillian.[15] It is a sea story, Melville's favorite genre. It deals with rebellion. It has reference to reforms, in this case impressment. It is rich in historical background, and concerns ordinary seamen. All those features of *Billy Budd* bear the stamp of the youthful Melville.

In one important respect, however, *Billy Budd* is different from almost all of Melville's other stories. It is written with a cool, detached pen, a seemingly impartial pen.[16] This odd development for Melville has had much to do with launching the "acceptance" theory.

In his preface to *Billy Budd*, Melville speaks of the impact of the French Revolution upon the British Navy, and passes both favorable and unfavorable judgment as to its effects. But, in speaking of the sailors and their conditions of life — Melville's strongest interest — he says:

> ... it was something caught from the Revolutionary Spirit that at Spithead emboldened the man-of-war's men to rise against real abuses. ... the Great Mutiny [later at Nore], though by Englishmen naturally deemed monstrous at the time, doubtless gave the first latent prompting to most important reforms in the British Navy.

Thus the scene is set, and though Melville uses a cool pen, he is the Melville of old; his heart still beats quickly for the men in the heat and sweat of the hold.[17]

The main character of the piece, Billy Budd, is regarded judiciously by Melville. He is "at least in aspect" the "Handsome Sailor . . . a superior figure of [his] own class [accepting] the spontaneous homage of his shipmates . . . a nautical Murat" per-

---

[14] Matthiessen, *op. cit.*, p. 514.

[15] Mumford, *op. cit.*, p. 338, says: "Billy Budd contain[s] the earlier themes of . . . [Melville's] life, now transformed and resolved."

[16] Melville had once before used a seemingly impartial pen. "Benito Cereno" is a tale of irony.

[17] It is instructive to observe how Melville reworked his background source, *The Naval History of Great Britain*, by the British naval historian, William James, into a defense of the mutinying sailors at Spithead and Nore (Freeman, *op. cit.*, pp. 39-40).

haps. He could be "Ashore . . . the champion; afloat the spokesman; on every suitable occasion always foremost." Billy Budd
could be all these things, but he fails actually to become them.
Physically he is well suited for the role, but he is found wanting
mentally. Unperceptive, in fear of authority, extremely naïve,
suffering the tragic fault of a stammer in moments of stress, Billy
Budd cannot qualify as a *spokesman.* Melville lets us know this
early in the story, and keeps reminding us that "welkin-eyed"
Billy is nicknamed "Baby Budd," and is "young and tender" with
a "lingering adolescent expression." He is "a novice in the com-
plexities of factious life," so simple-minded that when asked by
an officer about his place of birth, he replies, "Please, Sir, I don't
know. . . . But I have heard that I was found in a pretty silk-
lined basket hanging one morning from the knocker of a good
man's door in Bristol." Melville warns us that Billy Budd "is not
presented as a conventional hero."

Melville regards Billy fondly, admiringly in many respects, but
critically. He reminds us of Billy's limitations throughout the tale,
so when Billy utters those famous words, "God bless Captain
Vere," the reader should be qualified to evaluate those words in
the mouth of the speaker.

Billy is an ironic figure, as is Captain Vere. Scholarly, retiring,
ill at ease with people, "Starry" Vere is in command of a ship at
war. Painfully aware of the evil in Claggart, and pronouncing
Billy's killing of him the blow of an "angel," Vere nevertheless
forces through the death sentence against Billy. A student of
philosophy, he ironically rules out all inquiry into the motives for
Billy's act and insists that he be tried for striking and killing a
petty officer, an approach that can only result in Billy's hanging
under the naval code. At heart a kind man, Vere, strange to say,
makes possible the depraved Claggart's wish — the destruction of
Billy. "God bless Captain Vere!" Is this not piercing irony? As
innocent Billy utters these words, does not the reader gag? The injustice of Billy's hanging is heightened by his ironic blessing of the
ironic Vere.

Herein lies the literary importance of the tale. The aged Melville had developed a new weapon in his lifelong fight against
injustice. Charles R. Anderson put it very well:

> The earlier Melville would have railed against the "evil" of such
> a system [the hanging of Billy], and the "inhumanity" of Vere be-
> ing willing to serve as a vehicle of it. . . . This is the wonder, the
> thing that makes *Billy Budd* significant, since Melville discovered

so little along this line—that irony is a subtler and finer device for the fiction writer than headlong attack on social abuses.[18]

Billy Budd gives us added proof of Melville's great capacity for growth as a writer. However, his development of a new tool had its ironic counterpart in Melville criticism; many critics mistook Melville's irony for a change in his thinking, rather than a richer development in his craft.

F. Barron Freeman, rejecting the "Testament of acceptance" theory, has substituted the "Recognition of necessity" theory. In an intensive study of the aged Melville's thought, Freeman finds "a calm acceptance of the necessity of earthly imperfection and original sin." In Billy, Freeman sees a "Christian hero" practicing resignation and achieving final, heavenly reward. To Freeman the "importance . . . in the tale of *Billy Budd* lies in the optimistic way in which it suggests an acceptance of Fate."[19]

Thus it becomes clear that Freeman's "Recognition of necessity" theory is not greatly different from the older "Testament of acceptance" theory. In both cases the rebellious Melville ends his days "chastened and subdued." Gone are the mad tossings of the *Pequod*, moored are the homesick soliloquies of Starbuck, in ashes are the beautiful wild fires of the "hot old man," Ahab. The aged Melville became reconciled. To Watson, Weir, Mumford, Sedgwick, and Thorp, it was achieved in bitterness. To Freeman it came happily in a rediscovery of traditional religious faith. In finally approving "the religious concept of earthly imperfection and heavenly goodness" the old sea dog had found his comfortable niche at the ancestral hearth. But Melville's complex tale offers a quite different theme for analysis as well.[20]

---

[18] From his critical comments upon reading this paper. Professor Anderson had begun approaching the irony in *Billy Budd* in his article, "The Genesis of *Billy Budd*," *American Literature,* XII, 329-346 (Nov., 1940).

[19] Freeman, *op. cit.,* pp. 115-124.

[20] Since this paper was begun, one critic has attacked the "Testament of acceptance" theory, while another has attacked Freeman's "Recognition of necessity" theory. Richard Chase says: ". . . it is my impression that Melville made his definitive moral statement in *Moby Dick, The Confidence Man,* and *Clarel,* and that the moral situation in *Billy Budd* is deeply equivocal." See his article, "Dissent on Billy Budd," *Partisan Review,* XV, 1212-1218 (Nov., 1948). Alfred Kazin, discussing Freeman's interpretation, says: "F. Barron Freeman . . . tries to blunt Melville's sharp edge. . . . did Melville make through Billy's rapturous death an affirmation of Christian belief? . . . In 'Billy Budd,' he [Melville] had obviously agreed to accept the whole mysterious creation at last, with the weariness of an old man for whom all questions of justice end in death. . . . But it does not follow from this that he forgave God for just possibly not existing." See his review, "Ishmael in His Academic Heaven," *New Yorker,* Feb. 12, 1949, 84-89.

Freeman sees in "the calm description of Billy's ascension" Melville's considered judgment of "hope and triumph in death. . . ."[21] Again, style, tone, and form are mistaken for content. For Billy's triumph is not personal; it is social, and so of this world.

As Billy stands on deck with the rope around his neck, "A meek shy light appeared in the East, where stretched a diaphanous fleece of white furrowed vapor. That light slowly waxed. . . ." About to die, Billy, who could not conceive of malice or ill will, offers his humble benediction to Vere. And here the main point of Melville's ironic tale is revealed. The sailors, brought on deck to witness the hanging, echo Billy's words. "Without volition as it were, as if indeed the ship's populace were the vehicles of some vocal current electric, with one voice from alow to aloft, came a resonant sympathetic echo — 'God bless Captain Vere.' " But this is not intended for Vere, for: "yet at that instant Billy alone must have been in their hearts, even as he was in their eyes." The men blessed Billy, not Vere, with the words "God bless Captain Vere." Though hanged as a criminal, Billy is lovingly remembered for his martyrdom. The bluejackets keep track of the spar from which Billy was suspended. "Knowledge followed it from ship to dock-yard and again from dock-yard to ship, still pursuing it even when at last reduced to a mere dock-yard boom. To them a chip of it was as a piece of the Cross." Billy dies in helpless defeat only to become ironically reincarnated as a living symbol for all sailors.

And finally Billy is immortalized in a ballad composed by his shipmates. It is a tender ballad, mournful and affectionate, and sings of identification of all sailors with Billy.

> . . . Through the port comes the moon-shine astray!
> . . . But 'twill die in the dawning of Billy's last day.
> A jewel-block they'll make of me to-morrow,
> . . . Like the ear-drop I gave to Bristol Molly—
> . . . Sure, a messmate will reach me the last parting cup;
> . . . Heaven knows who will have the running of me up!
> . . . But Donald he has promised to stand by the plank;
> So I'll shake a friendly hand ere I sink.
> . . . Sentry, are you there?
> Just ease these darbies at the wrist,
> And roll me over fair.
> I am sleepy, and the oozy weeds about me twist.

---

[21] Freeman, *op. cit.,* pp. 125-126.

Thus Billy becomes — under Melville's ironic pen — something he never intended becoming: a symbol to all bluejackets of their hardship and camaraderie. He stammered in life, but spoke clearly in death.

So ends Melville's last book, with the sailors singing "Billie in the Darbies," honoring him as one of their own. In this song Melville sings to bewildered Wellingsborough of *Redburn;* to Jack Chase, the Great Heart of *White-Jacket;* to Steelkilt of *Moby-Dick,* to all the breathing, bleeding characters he ever put on paper.

In *Billy Budd,* Melville presents a picture of depravity subduing virtue, but not silencing it. Billy is sacrificed, but his ballad-singing mates seize upon this as a symbol of their lives. They never accepted natural depravity as victor, and they lived to see the end of impressment.

Melville knew that. He wrote the story of mutinies in the British Navy almost a full century after they took place. He had the tremendous advantage of historical perspective, a fact almost all critics have overlooked. By 1888 one could correctly evaluate the events of 1797. Melville could appreciate the legacy of the impressed Billy Budds and their mates: "the Great Mutiny, though by Englishmen naturally deemed monstrous at the time, doubtless gave the first latent prompting to most important reforms in the British Navy."

Billy Budd, forcibly removed from the ship *Rights-of-Man,* helped bring the rights of man to the seamen of His Majesty's Navy. His shipmates aboard H.M.S. *Indomitable* made this possible, along with the generations of seafaring men who followed.

Richard Chase

From *Selected Tales and Poems* by Herman Melville

It is high praise indeed to speak of a story as just missing equality with the small body of great tragic literature. And that is how we nowadays think of *Billy Budd*, which Melville wrote in the years between 1888 and 1891, the year of his death. A comparison of *Billy Budd* with the *Antigone* of Sophocles can, I think, be taken just literally enough to point to the decisive difference of achievement.

Both works are concerned with the defeat by abstract legality of an individual who possesses in more than usual measure certain timelessly precious human attributes. If we mean by a tragic hero a man of high estate who falls from prosperity by a flaw in his character or because he is guided by a power beyond his control or because of a mistake he makes, we may say of both *Billy Budd* and *Antigone* that the tragic hero himself is of only secondary interest. In the formal structure of those works Captain Vere and Creon are tragic heroes; yet in each instance the author's main

From the Introduction by Richard Chase to *Selected Tales and Poems* by Herman Melville, ed. Richard Chase (New York: Holt, Rinehart and Winston, 1950), pp. xiii-xvi. Introduction copyright 1950 by Richard Chase. Reprinted by permission of Holt, Rinehart and Winston, Inc.

interest, his most abundant flow of emotion, is directed toward someone else; in Sophocles, it is Antigone; in Melville, Billy Budd. In both works, the tragic hero is personally superior to the legal ideology he believes he must enforce. The two characters are adequately conceived by their authors. But we must admit that Sophocles is more successful with his Antigone than is Melville with his Billy Budd. In Antigone's insistence on the proper burial of her dead brother we see the full lineaments of a marvelously rich and mature character and a profound commitment to certain sources of moral and spiritual health. In comparison with Antigone, we must see that Billy Budd is not quite adequately conceived for the part he is supposed to play, the part, that is, of innocence and generosity in tragic collision with the rigid proscriptions of society. In some ways at least, Billy Budd strikes us as not quite believable. There are contradictory elements in his character; he is, for example, "innocent," yet he has had "experience." We ought to desire the tragic writer to show us innocence as it has survived or been produced by experience, by knowledge of life. The mindless innocence of Billy Budd, like that of a child, is wonderfully touching and valuable. Yet it is not quite the stuff of tragedy. Melville, as we see, was not free of the vast commitment of the American Man to the American Boy.

Captain Vere is finely portrayed. Somewhat in the manner of Captain Delano, he is an admirable if (in relation to the ultimate possibility of human character) fundamentally second-rate man. Claggart is also perfectly imagined — a man depraved by nature and by "Cain's City."

I would suggest that the relative failure of Billy Budd as a fictional character can be accounted for in a very simple manner. Melville was too personally involved with Billy Budd. Whether he was picturing his own son Malcolm (who shot and killed himself at the age of twenty) or speaking of his own youth or of Christ or making a general statement of the perpetual sacrifice of boyish innocence to law and society, the idea of Billy Budd appeared so overwhelmingly moving to the aged Melville that he was not able to express it in artistically cogent language. If the reader wishes to look into the subterranean depths of the story, its "secret mines and dubious sides," he might well begin with the large number of figures of speech having to do with the act of eating; for example, the "mesmeric glance" of Claggart at Billy Budd, which Melville compares with "the hungry lurch of the torpedo fish." These metaphors show what Melville, in his darkest vision of life, is really saying. He is saying that the "horrible vulturism" of the world, of which he had written in *Moby Dick*, is a basic principle of things. Society, law, adulthood, worldly accomplishment can sustain themselves only by feeding on youthful innocence and generosity. In this sense, the theme of *Billy Budd*, as of Melville's *Typee*, and, indeed, as of the sacrament of communion, is the ritualistic sacrifice of the hero.

But even as Melville shows us these dark and terrible ideas, we are aware that he is counterposing another range of meaning. Neither nature nor society is totally destructive of what is admirable in human life. By some genial, liberating grace, innocence and beauty are empowered to renew themselves in the very teeth of destruction. And so we are enabled to feel that *Billy Budd*, though not quite successful as tragic drama, remains immensely moving as a drama of pathos and myth. In this respect, its kinship is with the late plays of Shakespeare and with the New Testament, in its affirmation that out of the death inflicted by nature and society there issues new life.

We have already noticed Melville's use of flower imagery to indicate the resurgence of genial powers, as in *Jimmy Rose* and *The Fiddler*. This will of course make clear the significance of the name, Billy Budd.

Melville is the most Shakespearean of American writers, a fact that will be brought home afresh to anyone who compares *Billy Budd* with such a play as *The Winter's Tale*.* Like *Antigone* and *Billy Budd*, *The Winter's Tale* is concerned with the destruction of innocence and beauty by an inhumanly enforced legality. It is jealousy and suspicion which immediately cause Leontes, King of Sicilia, to bring about the death of his queen, Hermione, and his son, Mamillius. But mirrored in the jealous king we see the proscriptions of society conspiring with the destructive powers of nature — though, like Creon and Captain Vere, Leontes is personally superior to the law he lives by. In the "welkin eye" of Mamillius and of Billy Budd (Melville borrowed the phrase from Shakespeare) we see the idyllic world of eternal boyhood — described as follows by Polixenes as he recalls his boyhood friendship with Leontes:

> We were as twinn'd lambs that did frisk i' the sun
> And bleat the one at th' other. What we chang'd

---

*A comparison brought in detail to my attention by Professor Andrew Chiappe.

Was innocence for innocence; we knew not
The doctrine of ill-doing, nor dream'd
That any did.

The hanging of Billy Budd, at once a death and a resurrection, has the same force in Melville's story as the resurrection of Hermione at the end of Shakespeare's play, for both writers affirm that in some magical way innocence and beauty still exist in the world, that however evil nature and man may be they are still graced with a kind of minimal creative principle. Claggart's death is sudden and final. Captain Vere dies without having achieved the fame that might otherwise have come to him. But "the fresh young image of the Handsome Sailor" lives on in the heart of men. Of Melville, of Shakespeare, and of Sophocles (in *Oedipus at Colonus*) it may be said that in the works of their advanced age they took up the themes of the pathos of death, the crimes of society, the magically creative and restorative powers of nature, the myth of rebirth.

Norman Holmes Pearson

"Billy Budd: 'The King's Yarn'"

Another American classic is being discovered in Herman Melville's *Billy Budd, Foretopman.* The delay in the general acceptance of *Moby-Dick* as a classic, from the time of its publication in 1851 until the nineteen-twenties, is only partially explicable. But that *Billy Budd,* on its posthumous publication in 1924, should not then have been equally hailed is not altogether surprising. *Billy Budd* was an old man's book, finished as a last testament five months before his death. "Gone," wrote its editor and his first modern biographer, "is the brisk lucidity, the sparkle, the verve. Only the disillusion abided with him to the last." The nineteen-twenties were not an old man's age. The intimations of immortality continued to be found in the unclouded intuitions and perceptions of the young, who were closest to nature. Ahab was not young, but the young liked him. He was all heart and no reason; conventions were an anathema to him. Briskness, sparkle, and vere, though perhaps not the precise words to characterize him,

From *American Quarterly,* III (Summer 1951), 99-114. Reprinted by permission of the author, and the publisher, the University of Pennsylvania. Copyright 1951, Trustees of the University of Pennsylvania.

were nevertheless akin to his anarchistic conduct. Ahab was not unsuited to the decade.

The nineteen-thirties made up a different chapter of history. The reliance on the power of the primitive senses as a means by which to win one's way through difficulty to freedom, gave way to the revolutionary strength of reason when applied technologically to the manipulation of the social group. There was a hopeful reliance that men acting together might achieve what the individual by himself could not. Sad as the world seemed in its breadlines, it was still no time for what Lewis Mumford in 1929 had called "the ultimate peace of resignation," or what Grant Watson in 1933 described as "the supreme quality of acceptance."

A literary classic is established by an age whose emotional needs it serves. Thereafter it may rest on its laurels, even if its function becomes emeritus. Melville's story of a young sailor, impressed on a man-of-war and hanged, without his complaint, by the letter of the law, has found its moment of laureation now in a time of increasing turmoil, a time when we seem to find our chief hope in Eliot's poems which hover between Good Friday and an Easter Sunday which never arrives. As a classic, *Billy Budd* may be more congenial to the needs of our moment than *Moby-Dick* is.

Yet the two books stand alongside each other. Perhaps in time they will seem to be parts of a single whole, as though a problem were presented by Melville first from one angle and then from another.

Moby-Dick is so dominated by the tormented figure of Captain Ahab that the book seems his story alone. It is his story, but it is also Ishmael's, whose university the *Pequod* became. *Moby-Dick* begins and ends with the inquisitive wanderer who is our surrogate. Given his sensibility and ours, his intelligence linked to our own, we can never hear the captain's name without being reminded of the wicked king of the Old Testament who "did evil in the sight of the Lord above all that were before him." Each time the word Ahab appears on the printed page the connotation is reaffirmed. Nor can the informed reader forget the echoes of King Lear in Ahab's torrential rhetoric. Combined with the wickedness of Ahab is the memory of Lear's folly, magnificent though that folly may have been. As both the son of Omri and Lear can be said to be studies in the responsibilities of kingship, so Ahab is a study in captaincy, presented for critical observation. Ishmael, remembering, may admire the Titanic force of his commander, but he can never forget what Ahab actually did to the world which was the ship in its passage out.

It was Father Mapple who, in that otherwise structurally extraneous speech, set Ishmael, at the beginning, the lesson to be pondered.

But oh! shipmates! on the starboard hand of every woe, there is a sure delight; and higher the top of that delight than the bottom of the woe is deep. Is not the main-truck higher than the kelson is low? Delight is to him — a far, far upward, and inward delight — who against the proud gods and commodores of this earth, ever stands forth his own inexorable self. . . . Delight is to him who gives no quarter in the truth, and kills, burns, and destroys all sin though he pluck it out from under the robes of Senators and Judges. Delight,—top-gallant delight is to him, who acknowledges no law or lord, but the Lord his God, and is only a patriot to heaven. Delight is to him, whom all the waves of the billows of the seas of the boisterous mob can never shake from this sure Keel of the Ages. And eternal delight and deliciousness will be his, who coming to lay him down, can say with his final breath — O Father! — chiefly known to me by Thy rod — mortal or immortal, here I die. I have striven to be Thine, more than to be this world's or mine own. Yet this is nothing: I have eternity to Thee; for what is man that he should live out the lifetime of his God?

If Ahab himself heard Father Mapple's sermon, he stopped with the command to kill, burn, and destroy. The critics in the nineteen-twenties seemed to stop there with him. But if Ishmael had seen all that we, in turn Ishmael's surrogates, can witness of Ahab with the Parsee in the pale phosphorescence, he would have known that Ahab was no patriot to heaven. *"Ego non baptizo te in nomine patris, sed in nomine diaboli!"* was the dedication of the harpoon. Ahab tossed away more than his pipe of comfort, and more too than the use of reason and knowledge which the quadrant and compass signified. Ahab had shifted ensigns.

Billy Budd is similarly presented for observation. Billy is the dominant figure, but his significance comes not through our vicarious identification with him. It is felt in terms of his effect upon others, chiefly among whom is Captain Vere. Billy's course is straightforward; Veer's problems are those we can share. Actually it is difficult to say whether the action of the book is primarily concerned with the conflict between Billy and Claggart, the master-at-arms who so falsely accuses him and whom Billy fells with a blow, or whether this is simply a preliminary to the relationship of Billy to Vere, and of Vere to his duties of command. The climax of the book is the hanging of Billy at the yard-arm for the blow he struck; and Billy's summary end is the decision of the captain. Yet the book does not conclude with the hanging, but with the effect of the hanging upon others. The last chapters may be, as Melville calls them, "ragged edges," but ragged or not they are part of the same cloth, the quality of any fragment of which, whether early or late, depends upon the whole.

It might be said that we should view *Billy Budd* or any verbal work of art by itself alone, without regard to its history. But no word or group of words exists without history. Whatever we have in the way of association we bring to them, whether we write them or read them. The associations are part of the final richness of texture. This the writer depends upon, or at least he may not escape. Melville, writing at the close of his life, would have found it as impossible to have written of a captain like Vere without recalling Ahab as it is for us to escape his memory, who almost inevitably come to the reading of *Billy Budd* with *Moby-Dick* already in mind. If to later readers the order is by some chance reversed, the mutual relationship will still remain. But to Melville, at least, the sequence was chronological. If *Moby-Dick* was not a source for *Billy Budd*, it was at any rate a resource, one of the many on which he drew, and with the knowledge of which we can most profitably read the result with its interwoven implications.

There was of course for *Billy Budd* what scholars call *"the source,"* a dominant stimulus in a revival of interest in the 'eighties in the episode of Midshipman Philip Spencer on board the brig *Somers*, which Charles R. Anderson has called to our scholarly attention, and the limits of which Newton Arvin has significantly extended in a later article. Spencer, with two others, was executed for mutiny in 1842, the technical accuser having been Melville's first cousin, whose later years were reported to have been consequently "moody, taciturn, and restless." Thurlow Weed's autobiography, as Arvin points out, gave in 1883 what was said by Weed to be a true account of the cousin's coercion by his captain to sustain the charge and secure conviction despite the doubts of the court of inquiry; lest there be, as the severity of the captain put it, "no security for the lives of officers or protection to commerce if an example was not made in a case so flagrant as this." "It is obvious," wrote Weed, ". . . that there was no necessity for or justice in the execution of the alleged mutineers, one of whom

[Elisha] Small, a great favorite with the crew, exclaimed, 'God bless the flag!' at the moment he was run up to the yard-arm."

This tells us something about *Billy Budd,* and gives a personal in addition to a general reason for Melville's preoccupation with the circumstances of an incident which he had mentioned in *White-Jacket* without identifying it. Weed's autobiography, however, brings the case closer to the data of *Billy Budd* than even our knowledge of Melville's cousinship does. We can see that Captain Mackenzie, of the *Somers,* acted somewhat in the manner of Captain Vere, of the *Indomitable.* Small, as the family name of a favorite sailor, is a diminutive like Budd. "God bless the flag!" rings close to the "God bless Captain Vere!" which was Billy's death-cry. But whether these are equivalents is another matter, for into *Billy Budd* went the melding of many other resources.

The material from *White-Jacket* was a component part. Since *Billy Budd* dealt with a similar *mise en scène* of life aboard a man-of-war, *White-Jacket,* like the experiences it relates, must have come naturally to his mind. In the crew of the *Neversink* was the physical duplicate of the aged Dansker, the mainmastman who served as Billy's "Delphic" counsellor. In *White-Jacket,* too, was the rôle of the master-at-arms. "He it is," Melville said, "whom all sailors hate. His is the universal duty of a universal informer and hunter-up of delinquents. On the berth-deck he reigns supreme; spying out all grease-spots made by the various cooks of the seamen's messes. . . ." Bland was his name, and, Melville wrote, "a studied observation . . . convinced me that he was an organic and irreclaimable scoundrel, who did wicked deeds as the cattle browse the herbage, because wicked deeds seemed the legitimate operation of his whole infernal organization. Phrenologically, he was without a soul." Claggart grew out of Bland, just as there was a relationship, though slighter, between Jack Chase, "our noble first captain of the top" and Billy Budd, whose story was dedicated to Chase. "Jack must have been a by-blow of some British admiral of the blue," Melville wrote in *White-Jacket;* while later, "Yes, Billy Budd was a foundling, a presumable by-blow, and, evidently, no ignoble one. Noble blood was as evident in him as in a blood horse." But over the good and the evil on board the *Neversink* and the *Indomitable* extended the shadow of the Articles of War. Though any sailor on the *Neversink* who was maligned by an officer might stir in anger, yet his "indignant tongue is treble-knotted by the law that suspends death itself over his head should his passion discharge the slightest blow at the boy-worm that spits at his feet." The *Neversink* was part of Melville's fleet. "As the man-of-war that sails through the sea," he wrote at the conclusion of *White-Jacket,* "so this earth that sails through the air." This was the same voyage of the *Pequod* and the *Indomitable.*

It was on such a voyage that Billy Budd was impressed, where a master-at-arms might serve as his petty-officer, but where the Honorable Edward Fairfax Vere was the true and ultimately responsible captain of the king's ship. As such, Vere stamped both boat and book with his character. Versed in the science of the sea, unlike Ahab he trusted knowledge, reason, and the quadrant and the compass. "He had seen much service, been in various engagements, always acquitting himself as an officer mindful of the welfare of his men, but never tolerating an infraction of discipline; thoroughly versed in the science of his profession, and intrepid to the verge of temerity, though never injudiciously so." One cannot help but wonder whether Melville did not actually partition the captain of the *Pequod* in writing his final book, retaining for Vere all that had been potentially good in Ahab, while giving to Claggart so much that was evil in him. "The monomania in the man," Melville says of Claggart as he might have said of Ahab — "this, like a subterranean fire, was eating its way deeper and deeper in him. Something decisive must come of it."

But Vere, like the book, was not all salt. Regarding him, "one would be apt to say," Melville puts it, "Between you and me now don't you think there is a queer streak of the pedantic running through him? Yes, like the King's yarn in a coil of navy-rope?" "Some apparent ground there was for this sort of confidential criticism," Melville continued,

> since not only did the Captain's discourse never fall into the jocosely familiar, but in illustrating any point touching the stirring personages and events of the time he would be as apt to cite some historic character or incident of antiquity [as] he would [to] cite from the moderns. He seemed unmindful of the circumstance that to his bluff company such remote allusions however pertinent they might really be were altogether alien to men whose reading was mainly confined to the journals.

Few books are as literary in texture and ultimate substance as *Billy Budd.* Like the King's yarn, that colored strand woven through cordage to denote it as the property of the crown, constant learned allusion threads its way through the fabric of Melville's tale, so integrated with the narrative that the architectonics of the

book depend as much upon the one as the other. Melville's book-
ishness was grossly apparent in *Mardi*, where he had tried to climb
Parnassus with a knapsack of learning. It is not absent in *Billy
Budd*, but the burden is lessened.

An early draft of *Billy Budd* has been discovered and published
by F. Barron Freeman. The plot, so to speak, is fully there; but
the novel with its unique quality is not. The process of Melville's
elaboration of the briefer version was not to increase the denota-
tive involvement of the plot, but, like one pondering a situation
and ruminating over it, to bring to bear in terms of cited relevancies all of the understanding gained through the long years of
his life, no matter whence the resources came. The result was not
decoration but an attempt at definition by analogy and extension.
The pace is slackened, the syntax sometimes tortured like a mind
painfully exact, but a new density is achieved.

"O Nature and O soul of man!" Melville wrote in *Moby-Dick*,
"how far beyond all utterances are your linked analogies! not the
smallest atom stirs or lives on matter, but has its cunning duplicate
in mind." By the pattern of these "linked analogies" a sustained
dimension is added to the simpler measurement of the surface
narrative. This is one manner of achieving depth. Melville knew
how to accomplish such manipulation, and much of the significance
of *Moby-Dick* comes from it. There, as has been suggested, behind
the captaincy of Ahab are the recurring and enforcing analogies
of the Old Testament and Shakespeare's tragedies. This is not a
matter of identity but of the establishment of significant relevance.
It is not simply that Melville asks *Moby-Dick* to be put on the
shelf of such company, but rather because his book will not be
understood without feeling what lurks, almost mythically, behind
the episodes of whaling. It is not difficult to see why *Moby-Dick*
displays its full nature only for the literate.

Billy Budd is similar. It has its true existence only on the
printed page, in combination with the sensibility and knowledge of
the reader responding to the implication of what is written in detail
as well as what is done. *Billy Budd* on the stage is only the early
draft stripped down a little more. For at every step of the novel,
Melville is at work in the manner of Vere. He, like Vere, brings
knowledge to bear, even on Billy himself, who was innocent and
without knowledge. Thus the incident aboard the *Indomitable* is no
isolated case. Its circumstances of mutiny are related by analogy
to the *Somers*, which had occasioned the book, but was now both
distinct and joined, and to the Spithead and the Nore mutinies. It

is even related to the Civil War, that mutiny within a state whose implications had been a troubled concern of some of Melville's poetry.

Other areas of reference and analogy appear, and especially among them is the nature of Lord Nelson, to whom a chapter of *Billy Budd* is devoted. Nelson's life was one of those books which a man like Vere might have taken aboard for companionship. Melville himself owned a copy of Southey's biography of this "greatest sailor since the world began," in which he marked passages for remembrance:

> "There are three things, young gentleman," said Nelson to one of his midshipmen, "which you are constantly to bear in mind. First, you must always implicitly obey orders, without attempting to form any opinion of your own respecting their propriety. Secondly, you must consider every man your enemy who speaks ill of your King; and, thirdly, you must hate the French as you do the Devil."

A sentiment from a letter by Nelson to the Duke of Clarence also held Melville's attention:

> To serve my King, and to destroy the French, I consider as the great order of all, from which the little ones spring. . . .

Such quotations seem almost as much *the* source as is the incident on the *Somers;* and there are other links between Nelson and Melville's novel, which Mr. Freeman has pointed out in his excellent introduction to the latest edition of *Billy Budd.* "These excerpts," he says, speaking of the two quotations above, and one other, "are of significance chiefly as an explanation of Captain Vere's attitude and ideas on duty and love of country." This they do, of course, and reaffirm the importance to Melville of that verse from Dibdin's sailor poems, which Melville quotes with such approval both in *White-Jacket* and in *Billy Budd:*

> And as for my life, 'tis the King's!

There is the danger of too strict a delimitation in Mr. Freeman's use of "chiefly." The French become more than a physical antagonist when we remember the referential nexus of Melville's scattered use of the French in terms of their involvement with the revolutionary spirit which lay, at least for him, behind the Great Mutiny itself. "Reasonable discontent," Melville wrote, "growing out of practical grievances in the fleet had been ignited into irrational combustion as by live cinders blown across the Channel from France in flames." A kind of disobedient godlessness had sprung up to accompany the instinctive assertion of the rights of man. The name of the *Athéiste*, which belonged to the French warship whose musket-ball was almost casually to kill Vere, signified more than its national registry. For it caught up the whole Voltairian spirit of the "invading waters of novel opinion, social, political, and otherwise, which carried away as in torrents no few minds in those days." The French Revolution, the great and little mutinies at sea, and the Civil War become somehow entangled. Speaking of Vere in lines which follow the last quotation, Melville wrote:

> While other members of that aristocracy to which by birth he belonged were incensed at the innovators mainly because their theories were inimical to the privileged classes, not alone Captain Vere disinterestedly opposed them because they seemed to him incapable of embodiment in lasting institutions, but at war with the peace of the world and the true welfare of mankind.

This was the generalized mutiny in which Vere was involved. As captain of the king's man-of-war, himself almost a man-of-war, he was loyal to "duty and love of country," but it was an enriched patriotism which shared in events before his life and later than he himself was to know. Vere remained, however, relevant to them all.

A wide span of history was involved in the complex of *Billy Budd*, but the yarn of pedantry encompassed literature as well in establishing relevancies. For just as behind the history of whaling in *Moby-Dick* were the "linked analogies" of the Old Testament and Shakespeare, so behind the historical data of *Billy Budd* was a similar use of the New Testament and Milton. The effect in both cases was to broaden the implication by calling upon associations. In the *"ego non baptizo te in nomine patris"* of the earlier book, which in terms of the added *"sed in nomine diaboli"* Melville called its secret motto, there was no place for the Son or the Holy Ghost when Ahab renounced the Father for the Devil. In *Billy Budd*, the Son finds his place in the scheme of things for man. In a very recent book, *Milton and Melville*, Mr. Henry F. Pommer has shown a good deal of the Miltonic influence throughout all of Melville's work. In her book *Melville's Use of the Bible*, Miss Nathalia Wright has done the same for the influence of the Testaments. But each book is in its way somewhat exclusive, without seeming to recognize all of the implications of the combination of the two in relation to Melville's motive in converting the king's yarn of pedantry into a method like that of Milton's Raphael, when Raphael said to Adam:

> and what surmounts the reach
> Of human sense, I shall delineate so,
> By lik'ning spiritual to corporeal forms,
> As may express them best. . . .
>
> (*P. L.,* V, 571-574.)

What Melville was doing was to try to give in as universalized a way as possible, not simply a discussion of the mutiny in which his cousin had been so unhappily involved, nor simply a conflict between good and evil in the world, but another redaction of the myth which had concerned Milton himself in the trilogy of his three major works. Though certainly not planned as a trilogy from the start, Milton's chief poems do nevertheless take up complementary questions which only their totality answers in full. It is on these terms that we may look at *Paradise Lost,* concerned with man's fall after a state of innocence, as though it were necessarily followed by a second part in *Paradise Regained,* where we have the pattern of man's redemption through the example of Christ; and in turn, though out of chronological Biblical sequence, by a third, *Samson Agonistes,* in which one man's redemption is at last achieved.

Thus when we read in *Billy Budd* of the relationship between Billy, Claggart, and Vere, we are given a situation analogous to, and dependent upon, Milton's poetry and the Bible which stood behind it. This is Melville's use of the earth as the shadow of Heaven. What must be remembered is that there is only a shadow, and that Melville establishes momentary resemblances rather than complete identities. Thus Billy may without conflict be like prelapsarian Adam; like Christ who took the fallen Adam's place to carry out the obedience Adam denied; and like Isaac in relation to Abraham. But Billy never loses his identity as a sailor. Claggart may be like Satan, the Arch-Enemy who would attempt to rule the earth after his own fall and man's, and yet retain his character as master-at-arms of the *Indomitable.* Vere, too, may bear the same relationship of ultimate command to an Adam-Christ and to a Satan, who was his renegade chevalier, that a captain of a man-of-war does to his men, in an analogy of captaincy to the authority of God which is without the blasphemous assumption of Godhead. These are simply shifting similitudes, which reënforce but do not tie down.

Melville openly contrives the *mystique* of innocence in the person of Billy Budd as pre-lapsarian Adam. Few readers have ignored it. The very name of Budd is by definition an undeveloped shoot or stem, a person or thing not yet mature. In appearance he is "welkin-eyed," as Milton's Adam has an "eye sublime." Billy is, as the captain of the merchantmen says, "my best man," "the jewel of 'em," as Milton's Adam is the "goodliest." Billy and Adam are both paragons of appearance. But Melville is also forthright. "By his original constitution," Melville says, "aided by the coöperating influences of his lot, Billy in many respects, was little more than a sort of upright barbarian, much such perhaps as Adam presumably might have been ere the urbane Serpent wriggled himself into his company." Of his beginning, Billy did not know. He was Adamic and original, seeming to contain his family in himself. His situation is, as Melville puts it, that of "one to whom not as yet had been proffered the questionable apple of knowledge."

But man had eaten the apple long before Billy's time, and Billy was an anomaly. The idea of Adam remained chiefly as an example of what had been lost, and of events which should not have occurred. His place was taken by Christ. In Milton's words for God to Christ:

> Be thou in Adams room
> The Head of all mankind, though Adam's Son.
> As in him perish all men, so in thee
> As from a second root shall be restor'd,
> As many as are restor'd, without thee none.
> His crime makes guiltie all his Sons, thy merit
> Imputed shall absolve them who renounce
> Thir own both righteous and unrighteous deeds,
> And live in thee transplanted, and from thee
> Receive new life. So Man, as is most just,
> Shall satisfie for Man, be judg'd and die,
> And dying rise, and rising with him raise
> His Brethren, ransom'd with his own dear life.
> So Heavenly love shal outdoo Hellish hate,
> Giving to death, and dying to redeeme,
> So dearly to redeem what Hellish hate
> So easily destroy'd, and still destroyes
> In those who, when they may, accept not grace.
> (*P. L.,* III, 285-302.)

"Who was your father?" the young Budd was asked. His ambiguous answer may be read in either of two ways, according to stress: "God *knows*, Sir"; (in mild expletive) or "*God* knows, Sir" (in certification). Though Billy's hands were yellowed by the tarbucket, as Christ's might have been calloused by carpentry, yet in both was "something suggestive of a mother eminently favored by Love and the Graces; all this strangely indicated a lineage in direct contradiction to his lot." "Noble descent was as evident in him as in a blood horse." Something has been added to the analogy of Billy Budd to the Jack Chase of *White-Jacket*. In answer to the query of the drumhead court-martial, Billy Budd's answer comes clear: "I have eaten the King's bread and I am true to the King." What sort of loyalty is involved? Above the Prince of Peace stands the King of Kings, as above the sailor who is also a "peacemaker" is the British monarch who rules by divine right. "I have taken communion and remain loyal to God" lurks as a paraphrase of Billy's patriotism. It is as though he recognized in the word "patriotism" the possibilities of the highest connotations of a Fatherland. Through Billy also, as through Christ, is made possible a

> Recover'd Paradise to all mankind,
> By one mans firm obedience fully tri'd
> Through all temptation, and the Tempter foil'd.
> In all his wiles, defeated and repuls't. . . .
>
> (*P. R.*, I, 3-6.)

The Tempter for Christ, in *Paradise Regained*, was Satan; and for Billy Budd it was the master-at-arms. In Claggart's character the prototype of Bland was extended to cover the "pale ire, envy and despair" of Satan at the moment when he approached the Garden of Eden for the temptation of man. The occasion of the quotation from Milton which Melville used as epigraph to the description of Claggart was extended to the prolonged temptation of Christ in the wilderness which Milton described in *Paradise Regained*. It was Satan who, among other lures, tempted Christ to join in revolt against the Eternal King by the promise of wealth. Claggart through an intermediary tried Billy with two guineas. "We are not the only impressed ones, Billy," the whisper came. "There's a gang of us. — Couldn't you — help — at a pinch?" Our knowledge of the involvement of *Billy Budd* with Milton supplies the implied answer Billy could not give in stuttering his angry denial. It was Christ's retort to a similar temptation:

> Yet he who reigns within himself, and rules
> Passions, Desires, and Fears, is more a King;
> Which every wise and vertuous man attains:
> And who attains not, ill aspires to rule
> Cities of men, or head-strong Multitudes,
> Subject himself to Anarchy within,
> Or lawless passions in him which he serves. . . .
> Riches are needless then, both for themselves,
> And for thy reason why should they be sought,
> To gain a Scepter, oftest better miss't.
> (*P. R.*, III, 466-472, 484-486.)

It was Billy who struck the blow to the head that felled Claggart after the latter's false accusation of conspiracy in mutiny. Here in the accusation we have another of the analogies. When the temptation of the guineas is withstood, Miss Wright points out among her many Biblical parallelisms, "Claggart falsely charges that Billy is disloyal to the king. Only in this way, by treachery, can evil reach good. So Jesus was betrayed by Judas after he had resisted the temptations of Satan in the wilderness, and above him on the cross was hung the same charge, treason." So also is another distinct analogy when Vere exclaims over the dead body of Claggart: "It is the divine judgment of Ananias! . . . Struck dead by an angel of God." But Melville has not forgotten the resemblance to Milton's Satan, in describing Claggart as one, the touch of whose corpse was "like handling a dead snake." This blow at the head, this "capital wound," is the future consequence several times referred to in *Paradise Lost*, and again when Satan spoke in the opening lines of *Paradise Regained* to his cohorts:

>   well ye know
> How many Ages, as the years of men,
> This Universe we have possest, and rul'd
> In manner at our will th' affairs of Earth,
> Since Adam and his facil consort Eve
> Lost Paradise deceiv'd by me, though
> Since with dread attending when that fatal wound
> Shall be inflicted by the Seed of Eve
> Upon my head, . . .
> (*P. R.*, I, 47-55.)

But Billy is again like Christ when he will not defend himself before the judges, and is like Christ alone with God in Gethsemane when he has his moment with Vere in the cabin. So at the hanging, which inevitably reminds us of the Crucifixion, it is because of the cumulative analogies that we think beyond Billy Budd and his captain when we hear Billy's clear, unstuttered cry: "God bless Captain Vere." "Father, into thy hands I commend my spirit" is contained in it and echoes from it when "at the same moment it chanced that the vapory fleece hanging low in the East, was shot through with a soft glory as of the fleece of the Lamb of God seen in mystical vision and simultaneously therewith, watched by the wedged mass of upturned faces, Billy ascended; and ascending, took the full rose of the dawn." It is as though in addition to every-thing else which the king's yarn of special pedantry implied, the analogy of Abraham and Isaac, and God's pledge to Abraham, had fleetingly returned. We are brought back again, but without the loss of anything, to the realm of man where Billy Budd was a sailor, and Vere his commanding officer, on board a man-of-war whose interwoven cordage showed the H.M.S. *Indomitable* to be in the service of his Britannic Majesty as well as of the King of Kings.

Thus by widening arcs of transforming implication, Small's final cry, "God save the flag," aboard the *Somers*, has grown to meta-phorical dimensions, and, narrowing, been returned again. This is what Father Mapple called being a patriot to heaven. The cry of "O Father" in the final breath of Mapple's ideal hero joins him with Small, with Billy, and with Christ.

The story of the world which Melville tells in *Billy Budd* is the history of the future of man which Michael outlines to Adam in the final book of *Paradise Lost* and which serves as a kind of gloss to Melville's book. Mutiny as the ubiquitous metaphor in *Billy Budd* follows the archetypal pattern for fallen man established initially by the "rash revolt" of the angels against their King, and repeated by Adam and his consort. For this reason the Mosaic Code had been established, and for the same cause the stringent Articles of War prevailed. As Michael put it:

> therefore was Law given them to evince
> Thir natural pravitie, by stirring up
> Sin against Law to fight; . . .
> So law appears imperfect, and but giv'n
> With purpose to resign them in full time
> Up to a better Cov'nant, disciplin'd
> From shadowie Types to Truth, from Flesh to Spirit,
> From imposition of strict Laws, to free
> Acceptance of large Grace, from servil fear
> To filial, works of Law to works of Faith.
>
> (*P. L.*, XII, 287-289, 300-306.)

The test for the man who would stand upright again, as Billy stood and as Vere was to stand at Billy's execution, was in terms of law and of obedience. There was nothing for Billy to say in the end, but only to act obediently. His was the heroic example of innocence. His rôle was like that of Christ who had taken the fallen Adam's place.

The Honorable Edward Fairfax Vere was man as well as captain. He was *vir*, as Richard Chase suggests, as well as *veritas*. Unlike Billy, the apple of knowledge had been tasted by his lineage. His testing was of a different sort from Billy's, and of a kind closer to our own. Vere knew obedience, and for him reason was what Michael called "right Reason." Against this was the temptation of an allegiance to the heart and to the instincts, as Adam had bitten the fruit for love of Eve. To the original metaphor, Vere gives a new analogy as he reasons with the drumhead court to be firm.

> But the exceptional in the matter moves the heart within you. Even so too is mine moved. But let not warm hearts betray heads that should be cool. Ashore in a criminal case will an upright judge allow himself off the bench to be waylaid by some tender kinswoman of the accused seeking to touch him with her tearful plea? Well the heart sometimes the feminine in man, here is that piteous woman. And hard though it be, she must here be ruled out.

This is the temptation which Eve represented, redacted upon the otherwise womanless *Indomitable*. This is the victory which the first Adam had not won. It is Vere alongside Billy. As Vere had paced his cabin before addressing the jury, he was "without knowing it symbolizing thus in his action a mind resolute to surmount difficulties even if against primitive instincts strong as the wind and the sea." It was as though he rejected the pattern of Ahab who had acted only on instinct, and had swept aside our sympathy for a primitivism which could no longer be based on innocence. Vere, as captain, was his majesty's responsible deputy in a world of fallen man.

As such Vere lived, doing with obedience all that should be done. Should he not then, this model of post-lapsarian man, have been rewarded with long years of life and an admiralcy? "On the return passage to the English fleet," Melville wrote, "from the detached cruise during which occurred the events already recorded, the *Indomitable* fell in with the *Athéiste*. An engagement ensued; during which Captain Vere, in the act of putting his ship alongside the enemy with a view of throwing his boarders across the bulwarks, was hit by a musket-ball from a port-hole of the enemy's main cabin." He died, but as he died

> he was heard to murmur words inexplicable to his attendant — "Billy Budd, Billy Budd." That these were not the accents of remorse, would seem clear from what the attendant said to the *Indomitable's* senior officer of marines. . . .

That Melville's third principal character in the story should have died with Billy's name on his lips, is as important to understand as the significance of mutiny or Vere's surmountal of temptation. For on it depends the ultimate tone of the book, without which there could be no final definition. Billy Budd's death may seem to indicate how hard is the path of the beatitudes when followed in life. His story summarized in "an authorized weekly publication" meant nothing but the malformation of episodes which comes with time, and especially for those "whose reading was mainly confined to the journals." For the common sailors the yarn was woven into a popular ballad, and for a time the spar from which he was hanged was divided into chips like pieces of the Cross. "They recalled the fresh young image of the Handsome Sailor, that face never deformed by a sneer or subtler vile freak of the heart within!" The event was within their experience, and they understood it the better for that. Theirs was the final average reaction, as Billy's example drifted into time. The example might help, but actually they would need the "peacemaker" again in the midst, whether on board the merchantman or the man-of-war. Certainly they would still require captaincy like Vere's.

Most of all, remembering the king's yarn of pedantry, we ourselves will recall Vere with whom we, like Melville, might most closely identify ourselves. Vere is like a Samson Agonistes, who, having conquered the temptation of the senses and remained true to the will and reason, is redeemed. But unlike Samson, Vere is not given the destruction of the French to serve as substitute for the tumbled temple. Yet Vere, though his ambitions were not satisfied, and the spirit of mutiny would appear again, was not without his consolation. As post-lapsarian man, Vere has learned how to die, in his case by the example of a common sailor who was like a common carpenter. As the true Christian knows how to die in adversity with the peace which the name of Jesus brings to the lips, so "Billy Budd" is to Vere what "God bless Captain Vere" was to Budd.

They were "not the words of remorse." Both to Billy Budd, and to Vere by Budd's example, is that joy and success of true captaincy of which Father Mapple had spoken to Ishmael and to us. "Delight — top-gallant delight is to him who acknowledges no law or lord but the Lord his God, and is only a patriot to heaven." Now, though the King of Kings was known chiefly by his rod, is that which Ahab never found through his disobedience and renunciation of true reason for the temptation of the instincts. There was no top-gallant delight for him, as there was for the captain of an *Indomitable* or for a Billy Budd who was in every sense a true foretopgallantman.

This is the responsible pattern for fallen man, constantly subject to mutiny and such events as, to return to Melville's woven strand of pedantry, "converted into irony for a time those spirited strains of Dibdin":

> and as for my life, 'tis the King's!

"With mankind," Vere was accustomed to say, "forms, measured forms are everything; and that is the import couched in the story of Orpheus with his lyre spellbinding the wild denizens of the woods." "And this," as Melville states, "he once applied to the disruption of forms going on across the Channel and the consequences thereof."

Wendell Glick

"Expediency and Absolute Morality in *Billy Budd*"

"Resolve as one may to keep to the main road," Melville wrote in *Billy Budd*, "some bypaths have an enticement not readily to be withstood. Beckoned by the genius of Nelson, knowingly, I am going to err into such a bypath."[1] With these words of caution to the reader who might object to the "literary sin" of digression, the author of *Moby Dick* launched into a spirited encomium upon the heroism of Lord Nelson, defending the Admiral against any "martial utilitarians" and "Benthamites of war" who might interpret his acts of "bravado" at Trafalgar which had resulted in his death to have been foolhardy and vain. For what reason, the question arises, did Melville feel that the eulogy on Nelson could justifiably be included in *Billy Budd*? What is the meaning of the attack upon Benthamites and utilitarians? This was no pot-boiler which required padding; surely his inclusion of the highly emotional de-

---

Reprinted by permission of the Modern Language Association of America from *PMLA*, LXVIII (March 1953), 103-110. Copyright 1953, by the Modern Language Association of America.
[1] Herman Melville, *Billy Budd*, ed. F. Barron Freeman (Cambridge, Mass., 1948), p. 154n. Citations to *Billy Budd* in the text of this article are to this, the best critical edition so far available.

fense of Nelson is significant for other reasons than that the chapter makes "more understandable Melville's hearty interest in martial exploits, sayings, and songs."[2]

At the time Melville was writing and revising *Billy Budd* he was in no mood to trifle with peccadilloes. "My vigor sensibly declines," he had written to Archibald MacMechan on 5 December 1889: "What little of it is left I husband for certain matters as yet incomplete, and which indeed, may never be completed."[3] He could hardly have been husbanding his strength to communicate his "hearty interest in martial exploits"; his digression away from his narrative in order to praise Nelson must have served in his mind the more serious purpose of clarifying one of the "truths" for which, as he pointed out, *Billy Budd* was but the vehicle. The purpose of this article is to call attention to an aspect of one of these truths, heretofore unnoticed. Although it is much more, *Billy Budd* is the cogent fruition of a lifetime of observation and study of the eternal conflict between absolute morality and social expediency; and the digression on Nelson, though it intrudes upon the plot, is central to an understanding of Melville's final resolution of this crucial problem.

In writing *Billy Budd*, Melville made clear at the outset of his novel, he was writing no "romance"; he would not be bound, consequently, in his delineation of the "Handsome Sailor," by any of the conventions usually followed in depicting a romantic hero. Nor would he be bound to refrain from digressing if digression served his purposes. His interest was less in art than in "Truth uncompromisingly told" (pp. 149 and 274). He was quite willing, he asserted, to sacrifice "the symmetry of form attainable in pure fiction" and to risk "ragged edges" on his final work if by so doing he could tell a story "having less to do with fable than with fact" (p. 274). Thus relieved both from the conventional restrictions usually imposed by art and from the financial exigencies which had dictated the content of some of his early works, he would be free to deal forthrightly and honestly with issues far too serious to be treated cavalierly.

For his *raisonneur* Melville chose Captain "Starry" Vere, a clear-headed realist possessed of sufficient perspective as a result of broad human experience and extensive reading to enable him to weigh the most difficult alternatives and choose rationally between

---

[2] For this reason, Freeman suggests, the digressions on Nelson are "important" (p. 42).

[3] Leon Howard, *Herman Melville* (Berkeley, 1951), p. 328.

them. No person with lesser qualifications would serve. For the choice which Captain Vere had to make involved more than a simple distinction between blacks and whites; instead it was a choice between two standards of human behavior, to each of which man owed unquestioning loyalty. The Captain's decision, moreover, was to be Melville's as well; and Melville felt no disposition in the waning years of his life to trifle with reality and call the process truth-seeking.

Melville sympathized with Billy Budd as completely as did Captain Vere. He appreciated with the Captain the stark injustice of a situation which finds the individual condemned for adherence to a standard of behavior most men would consider noble and right. But he agreed with the Captain that justice to the individual is not the ultimate loyalty in a complex culture; the stability of the culture has the higher claim, and when the two conflict, justice to the individual must be abrogated to keep the order of society intact. Turning their backs upon one of the most cherished systems of ideas in the American tradition, a system typified by such individualists as Thoreau and Emerson, Melville and Captain Vere brought in the verdict that the claims of civilized society may upon occasion constitute a higher ethic than the claims of "natural law" and personal justice (p. 245). The ultimate allegiance of the individual, in other words, is not to an absolute moral code, interpreted by his conscience and enlivened by his human sympathies, but to the utilitarian principle of social expediency.

To isolate his problem, to strip it of all irrelevant issues preparatory to making a critical examination of it, Melville chose as his setting a British vessel at sea. The ship-of-the-line *Indomitable*, a smooth-functioning microcosm of society as a whole, was threatened with mutiny. Though the threat was remote, whatever would contribute to the end of knitting together the diverse individuals who made up the crew into a homogeneous unit which would act efficiently in an emergency was fully justified; conversely, that which jeopardized even slightly the clock-like functioning of the crew it was necessary to stamp out ruthlessly. His highest obligation, as Captain Vere conceived of it, was the preservation of the tight little society into which the crew had been welded, and the prevention of anything resembling anarchy. The transcendent responsibility of the leaders of the English nation, moreover, was the same as his own, writ large. An intensive study of history had confirmed his "settled convictions" against "novel opinion, social, political, and otherwise, which carried away as in a torrent no few minds in those days"; and he was "incensed at the innovators," not because their theories were inimical to the private interests of the privileged classes of which he was a member, but because such theories "seemed to him incapable of embodiment in lasting institutions," and "at war with the peace of the world and the true welfare of mankind" (pp. 163-64). The world as he viewed it was ruled by "forms"; "with mankind," Melville quotes him as saying, "forms, measured forms are everything"; that was the import which he saw "in the story of Orpheus with his lyre spellbinding the wild denizens of the woods" (p. 272). To preserve the ordered functioning of his crew Captain Vere was willing to sacrifice even the ideal of justice when the absolute necessity arose. What he objected to in Claggart was not that Claggart was remiss in his "duty of preserving order" but that the Master at Arms abridged the ideal of justice unnecessarily, even when the autonomy and general good of the crew were not at stake. Still, the maintenance of order came first, and it was rigorously safeguarded on the *Indomitable* "almost to a degree inconsistent with entire moral volition" (pp. 172-173).

To the idea that order in society should be maintained at all cost Captain Vere adhered "disinterestedly," not because he desired such a regimented society, but because he believed it to be a practical necessity of this world. Like Plotinus Plinlimmon of *Pierre*, he preferred Christian ("Chronometrical") standards of absolute morality to the more mundane, utilitarian standard of expediency; but like Plinlimmon, he had concluded that Christian ideals were unworkable in everyday situations. He was fully aware that a regimented society abridged many private rights, but he realized also that in the absence of such a society a state of anarchy and chaos inevitably arose in which every human right was sacrificed. An ordered society at least guaranteed the preservation of *some* rights; and though this fell far short of the ideal of the preservation of *all*, it was far better than the sort of "society" which, in the idealistic attempt to guarantee all rights, degenerated into chaos and so permitted their complete and total destruction. It was not a question of insuring all individual rights or a part of them; the choice was between insuring a part of them or none. The ideal society which abridged no prerogatives and guaranteed all private liberties was, in the considered opinion of Captain Vere, a figment of the imagination.

Recent events, Melville makes abundantly plain, had been responsible for the Captain's position. The Nore Mutiny, though it had been precipitated by the failure of the authorities to redress the legitimate grievances of the seamen, had threatened the military usefulness of the "indispensable fleet" upon which the stability of the entire English nation depended, and consequently had been ruthlessly suppressed (pp. 150-153). The cataclysmic French Revolution had taught its bitter lesson, both to Captain Vere and to his creator. To the Captain the principle involved in the two events was the same: the English sailors at Nore, in running up "the British colors with the union and cross wiped out," had transmuted "the flag of founded law and freedom defined" into "the red meteor of unbridled and unbounded revolt" of the French. "Reasonable discontent," Melville pointed out, "growing out of practical grievances in the fleet had been ignited into irrational combustion as by live cinders blown across the Channel from France in flames" (p. 151). No price was too great to pay to keep such unhinging forces of anarchy in check; in giving his life to destroy the *Athéiste,* Captain Vere sacrificed himself in defense of the *sine qua non* of civilized existence and in opposition to the false, unworkable doctrines of the French Revolution. The triumph of the *Indomitable* over the *Athéiste* was the triumph of order over chaos.

Yet how staggering was the cost of a stable society! Having decided upon the absolute necessity for maintaining unweakened the strength of the social fabric, Melville shuddered when he contemplated the price exacted in terms of human values; and *Billy Budd* became the balance-sheet upon which he reckoned the price men have to pay for the ordered society which they have to have. The most obvious price was the destruction of "Nature's Nobleman," the superlatively innocent person: every Billy Budd impressed by an *Indomitable* is forced to leave his *Rights-of-Man* behind. To the destruction of innocent persons, moreover, it was necessary to add the mental suffering of the individual forced to make moral judgments. But the total cost is not met even by the sacrifice of Billy Budds and the suffering of Captain Veres; social stability based upon expediency is paid for also with a general, blighting, human mediocrity. The standards of any civilized society are the standards of the great mass of men who make up its bulk; and when maintenance of the stability of society becomes the supreme obligation of every person, the result is a levelling of the superior persons down to the level of the mass. The chief personal virtue becomes "prudence"; the end most worth seeking for becomes "that manufacturable thing known as respectability," so often allied with "moral obliquities" (p. 147), and occasionally, as in the case of Claggart, indistinguishable even from "natural depravity." "Civilization," Melville remarks categorically, "especially if of the austerer sort, is auspicious" to natural depravity because natural depravity "folds itself in the mantle of respectability" by avoiding "vices or small sins" and by refraining from all excesses; in short, by exhibiting the prudence which is the only virtue society demands. The natural depravity of Claggart was so insidious because it lacked the trappings in which society expects to see evil garbed, and instead, prudently enfolded itself in "the mantle of respectability" (pp. 185-186). Prudence, while being the mark of the socially adjusted man who rigidly adheres to the utilitarian principle of expediency, may also be the last refuge of scoundrels.

But even when prudence did not take the extreme form of moral obliquity, even when it was not "habitual with the subtler depravity" (p. 195), as it proved to be in the case of Claggart, it left its mark upon the people in the world of Billy Budd. The most "prudent" characters discharged faithfully their "duty" to their king even when to do so clashed with moral scruple, but they fell far short of the personal heroism which inspires others and vitalizes them into acts. Captain Graveling of the *Rights-of-Man* was "the sort of person whom everybody agrees in calling 'a respectable man' "; he was a lover of "peace and quiet" and the possessor of "much prudence" which caused "overmuch disquietude in him," but he was by and large a pedestrian individual who could hardly be depended upon to make any signal contribution to human progress (p. 137). The old ascetic Dansker had learned from experience a "bitter prudence" which had taught him never to interfere, never to give advice, in other words, to solve the problem of his social responsibility by escaping into a shell of cynicism, and by so doing had disqualified himself for service to society (p. 205). The *Indomitable's* "prudent surgeon" was singularly unequipped to pass moral judgments and would have "solved" the problem of Billy's murder of Claggart by dropping the whole affair into the lap of the Admiral (pp. 229, 231). Even Captain Vere, who possessed in eminent measure the "two qualities not readily interfusable" demanded of every English sea-commander at the time "prudence and rigor" (p. 234), did not earn Melville's highest accolade as a member of "great Nature's nobler order" until he let himself "melt back into what remains primeval in our formalized humanity"; in short, until he forgot temporarily his "military duty," his prudence, and acted in a manner difficult to reconcile with strict social expediency (p. 252).[4]

---

[4] Melville conjectures that this is what transpired while the Captain spoke with Billy privately in the cabin.

To what do these examples of prudence, the highest ethic of utilitarian philosophers, add up? Simply this: in making social expediency an ethic superior to absolute morality, Melville found himself pushed perilously close to a *Weltanschauung* which would admit slight, if any, possibility of personal greatness. Could prudence ever be truly heroic? A society which elevated prudence above all other virtues seemed to be anathema to the sort of moral adventuresomeness which Melville loved, and which for him set the great man off from the mediocre one. Yet such a society seemed to be the only sort which could safeguard men from the perils of "irrational combustion" which followed hard upon an idealism permitted to run its free course unrestrained. Here lay a crucial dilemma: was the race doomed to accept mediocrity as the price of its self-preservation, or was it still possible in a complex society for great private virtues to generate and grow?

Emotionally unequipped to reconcile himself to the bleaker alternative toward which both his experience and his reason had led him, Melville turned to history in the hope of discovering a figure of heroic dimensions whose life would free him from his impasse. Having played the role of champion of man's dignity and greatness for a lifetime, he did not feel that he could relinquish it now; and in the person of Nelson, "the greatest sailor since the world began," he found his answer.[5] Though he recognized that many changes had taken place since Trafalgar, that the "symmetry and grand lines" of Nelson's *Victory* seemed obsolete in a world of "*Monitors* and yet mightier hulls of the European iron-clads," he nonetheless insisted that "to anybody who can hold the Present at its worth without being inappreciative of the Past," the "solitary old hulk at Portsmouth" spoke eloquent truth. If he could no longer embrace the simple faith of his youth when he had believed in a law "coeval with mankind, dictated by God himself, superior in obligation to any other," when he had advocated the abolition of flogging on the grounds that "it is not a dollar-and-cent question of expediency; it is a matter of *right and wrong*";[6] if the corrosive years had eaten away for him such immutable standards, he could at least salvage somehow a foundation for personal greatness and heroism. Nelson was the man he needed.

He admitted that strict "martial utilitarians," believers in the rigorous application of an inexorable social expediency to every

[5]The scattered references to *Billy Budd* which follow are to Ch. iv, pp. 154-157, passim.
[6]*White-Jacket* (Boston, 1892), pp. 138, 139.

particular situation, would be inclined to take issue with his estimate of Nelson's greatness, even perhaps "to the extent of iconoclasm." For Nelson's exposure of his own person in battle at Trafalgar appeared on the surface to have been militarily inexpedient, even vain and foolhardy; his value to the cause for which he fought was so great that he should have sacrificed his natural desire for personal heroism to the higher principle of preserving a life which was indispensable to the general good. Had his life been preserved and his command of the fleet therefore been retained, the mistakes made by his successor in command might have been avoided; and his sagacity might well have averted the shipwreck with its horrible loss of life which followed the battle. So the "Benthamites of war" argued, and, Melville admitted, with some plausibility; using only the immediate circumstances of the engagement as their criteria they could convict Nelson of behavior out of harmony with the general good, and on these grounds strip him of the glory with which Englishmen had invested him.

But to this sort of iconoclasm Melville would not accede for a moment. "Personal prudence," he countered, "even when dictated by quite other than selfish considerations is surely no special virtue in a military man; while an excessive love of glory, exercising to the uttermost heartfelt sense of duty, is the first."* The Benthamites were wrong; in applying their principle of social expediency to Nelson's deed "of foolhardiness and vanity" they failed to calculate the strength of purpose which such a "challenge to death" injects into the arteries of a nation. Nelson's deed was "expedient" to a degree they lacked the vision to perceive; his name had become a "trumpet to the blood" more stimulating even to the hearts of Englishmen than the name of Wellington; the act which on the surface seemed sheer "bravado" still inspired posterity to deeds of greatness.

Unless, Melville argued, Nelson's "challenge to death" could be considered an act of supreme heroism, conformable to the highest ideals governing human behavior, no deed could be truly heroic; and this possibility he refused to entertain. The vitality of Nelson's example was immortal. In 1891, shortly after he had made his own will, Melville composed this enthusiastic tribute to another great man who had also glimpsed a premonition that death was near:

---

*[This quotation actually follows Weaver's text, not Freeman's. Freeman's edition reads, ". . . glory, impassioning a less burning impulse the honest sense of duty, is the first."—EDITOR.]

At Trafalgar Nelson on the brink of opening the fight sat down and wrote his last brief will and testament. If under the presentiment of the most magnificent of all victories to be crowned by his own glorious death, a sort of priestly motive led him to dress his person in the jewelled vouchers of his own shining deeds; if thus to have adorned himself for the altar and the sacrifice were indeed vainglory, then affectation and fustian is each more heroic line in the great epics and dramas, since in such lines the poet but embodies in verse those exaltations of sentiment that a nature like Nelson, the opportunity being given, vitalizes into acts. (p. 157)

The question naturally arises whether Melville intended the digression on Nelson to illuminate the final scene of the novel. Might the answer be that the hanging of Billy Budd is Melville's final commentary upon the theme of the impracticability of absolute standards in a world necessarily ruled by expediency? Billy's noble devotion to absolute justice and right throughout the novel made him a sort of personification of the moral law; his death must have meant for Melville, consequently, that the standard of behavior to which Billy gave his allegiance, though a noble one, is simply unworkable when applied to complex social relationships. There was something unearthly about the death of Billy Budd: he was "an angel of God" (p. 229), returning without fear to his Maker; his pinioned figure at the yard-end behaved like that of no mortal man; to the sailors aboard the *Indomitable* the spar from which Billy's body had hung was thought of for some years as a piece of the Cross. The luminous night of the morning when Billy was to be hanged passed away like the prophet Elijah disappearing into heaven in his chariot and dropping his mantle to Elisha. Billy was too good for this world; he properly belonged to another, not to this; and the moral principles from which he acted were appropriate enough for the world to which he belonged. But in a society composed of men, not angels — in a society in which even Claggarts are to be found — an inferior standard, that of expediency, is the only workable one.[7]

---

[7] This article is peripheral to a study of the concept of "expediency" in American thought, undertaken with the aid of a grant from the American Council of Learned Societies.

R. W. B. Lewis

From *The American Adam*

The new Adam . . . is the Lord from heaven [ST. PAUL, I Cor. 45–47].

At least one of Melville's critics has found Homer's *Odyssey* a broad metaphor useful not only for gauging Melville's novels but also for describing his life. Toward the end of that life, W. H. Auden says in his poem "Herman Melville":

> he sailed into an extraordinary mildness,
> And anchored in his home and reached his wife
> And rode within the harbour of her hand,
> And went across each morning to an office
> As though his occupation were another island.
>
> Goodness existed: that was the new knowledge
> His terror had to blow itself quite out
> To let him see it; but it was the gale had blown him
> Past the Cape Horn of sensible success
> Which cries: "This rock is Eden. Shipwreck here."

From *The American Adam: Innocence, Tragedy, and Tradition in the Nineteenth Century* (Chicago: University of Chicago Press, 1955), pp. 146-152. Reprinted by permission of The University of Chicago Press. © The University of Chicago, 1955.

Mr. Auden's poem, which outlines Melville's life perhaps a shade too tidily by means of the Homeric allusions, has to do with the final tranquillity and the firm concluding Christian acquiescence out of which — according to Mr. Auden — Melville composed *Billy Budd.*

> . . . now he cried in exultation and surrender
> "The Godhead is broken like bread. We are the pieces."
> And sat down at his desk and wrote a story.

Melville's cry about "the Godhead" was in fact uttered in 1851, in the letter responding to Hawthorne's praise of *Moby-Dick*, some forty years before Melville sat down at his desk in New York and wrote Billy's story. But *Billy Budd* is, of course, unmistakably the product of aged serenity; its author has unmistakably got beyond his anger or discovered the key to it; and it would be pointless to deny that it is a testament of acceptance, as Mr. Watson has said, or a "Nunc Dimittis," as Mr. Arvin proposes. It is woeful, but wisely, no longer madly. Its hero is sacrificially hanged at sea, but its author has come home, like Odysseus.

In Melville's last work, the New World's representative hero and his representative adventure receive a kind of sanctification. Mr. R. P. Blackmur has said of the last three novels of Henry James that they approach the condition of poetry, which Mr. Blackmur explains as the exemplification in language of the soul in action — "the inner life of the soul at the height of its struggle, for good or evil, with the outer world which it must deny, or renounce, or accept." This, precisely, is what *Billy Budd* asks us to say about it; *Billy Budd* helps us to see that the action so described is one grounded in the pressures and counterpressures not of any world but of the New World. It is the action of the soul in general as shaped under a New World perspective. Melville's achievement was double: he brought myth into contemporary life, and he elevated that life into myth — at once transcending and reaffirming the sense of life indicated by the party of Hope.

Compare, for example, the personality and the career of the Handsome Sailor with the analysis of historic American Adamism offered by Horace Bushnell in 1858. Billy is innocence personified — "To be nothing more than innocent!" Claggart exclaims, in malice and tears. He can neither read nor write, though he can sing like an angel. He springs from nowhere; he returns a cheerful "No, sir," to the officer's question, "Do you know anything about your beginning?" "His entire family was practically invested in

himself." He fulfills every hopeful requirement; no historic process
or influence intrudes between him and the very dawn of time; his
defining qualities seem to be "exceptionally transmitted from a
period prior to Cain's city and citified man."

So it can be said of him that he "was little more than an upright barbarian, much such as Adam presumably might have been
ere the urbane Serpent wriggled himself into his company," and
that "in the nude [he] might have posed for a statue of Adam
before the Fall." This is just the personality that Bushnell saw
his culture fostering and which he deplored. Even Billy's stammer
and his illiteracy are integral to the portrait: they are the evidence
of that "condition privative," they constitute that "necessary defect of knowledge and consequent weakness" which Bushnell as-
signed to any "free person or . . . power considered as having just
begun to be." The defect and the weakness, under Claggart's goad-
ing, precipitate the disaster; and Billy falls, as the mythological
Adam had fallen, and as Bushnell foresaw that any Adamic American would fall. The myth enters into the life and reenacts itself:
but not at the expense of the life. Bushnell invoked the myth in order to chastise the tendencies of life in his day. But if Melville
celebrates the fall, he also celebrates the one who fell; and the
qualities and attitudes which insure the tragedy are reaffirmed in
their indestructible worth even in the moment of defeat. Melville
exposed anew the danger of innocence and its inevitable tragedy;
but in the tragedy he rediscovered a heightened value in the innocence.

Melville's achievement, as in *Moby-Dick*, was an artistic achievement, and it may be measured by the failure of *Pierre*, more than
three decades earlier. For the action fumbled with in *Pierre* is essentially the same as that of *Billy Budd*. From the moment on the
novel's first page when we are introduced to a "green and golden
World" and see young Pierre on a "morning in June . . . issuing
from the embowr'd . . . home of his fathers . . . dewily refreshed
and spiritualized by sleep," we know where we are and what and
whom we have to deal with. The very language contains strong
verbal echoes of Whitman's most explicit Adamic verse:

> As Adam, early in the morning,
> Walking forth from the bower refresh'd with sleep. . . .

The story of Pierre Glendinning consists in the explosion of
what Dr. Murray has called "this myth of paradise" — an explo-

sion resulting from an unpreparedness for the subsequent myth of the Fall; and in the explosion both the book and its hero are blown to pieces. It is not the hero who is at fault; he is not obliged to be prepared, his condition forbids it. But we have the impression that the hero's inventor was unprepared: he is not less shocked than Pierre when he sees what he says. The symbolic distance accomplished in *Moby-Dick* narrows fatally in *Pierre*; and if ever there was a case of symbolic suicide in literature, it is Melville's in the indiscriminate destruction in the concluding pages of *Pierre*. The myth which had been an ambiguous source of strength in *Moby-Dick* has now overwhelmed the life. And so in *Clarel*, Melville's next extensive piece of writing, we are not surprised to find an imagination winding its way through a maze of wasteland imagery, quite explicitly lamenting the bewildering and painful loss of Eden.

The recovery in *Billy Budd* is astonishing. The entire story moves firmly in the direction of a transcendent cheerfulness: transcendent, and so neither bumptious nor noisy; a serene and radiant gladness. The climax is prepared with considerable artistry by a series of devices which, though handled somewhat stiffly by a rusty creative talent, do their work nonetheless. The intent of all of them is to bring into being and to identify the hero and his role and then to institute the magical process of transfiguration. Billy appears as another Adam: thrust (like Redburn and Pierre) into a world for which his purity altogether unfits him. His one ally, the Danish sailor who is the prophetic figure in the story, eyes Billy with "an expression of speculative query as to what might eventually befall a nature like that, dropped into a world not without some man-traps and against whose subtleties simple courage lacking experience and address and without any touch of defensive ugliness, is of little avail; and where such innocence as man is capable of does yet in a moral emergency not always sharpen the faculties or enlighten the will."[1]

The Dansker carries the burden of awareness within the *novella* — awareness that "the matter of Adam" is being tested again; and the atmosphere grows thick with echoes of *Paradise Lost*. But all the time, other energies are linguistically at work. Melville sets

---

[1] *Melville's Billy Budd,* p. 177. Mr. Freeman, the editor, observes in a footnote that Melville wrote "an expression of speculative *foresight,*" then changed the final word to "query." It is instructive to watch, with Mr. Freeman's scholarly aid, as Melville subdues his more explicitly ritualistic language to the more realistic and dramatic.

swirling around his hero other allusions which relate Billy by infer-
ence to other beings: splendid animals, Catholic priests, royalty,
the gods — Apollo, Hercules, Hyperion. It is the destiny of these
figures to suffer transfiguration, to die into their sacrificial coun-
terparts — the sacrificial bull, the "condemned Vestal priestesses,"
the slain monarch, and the dying god. This is the process by which
Adam changes into the "new Adam" of St. Paul — "the Lord from
heaven." The value of the American Adam is thereby, at last,
transvalued.

The process is both complicated and enhanced by the ironically
entitled "digression" on Lord Nelson. The story of the common
sailor is suddenly stretched into great drama by a glimpse of the
"heroic personality" of "the greatest sailor since the world began."
Nelson, too, is killed at sea; and Melville anticipates the quality of
Billy's death by investing Nelson, at the moment of *his* "most
glorious death," with "a priestly motive," which led him to adorn
himself as "for the altar and the sacrifice." The classical drama of
the heroic nobleman points up the little adventure of the stammer-
ing and illiterate orphan; and Melville gets back to that adventure
by remarking that profoundest passion does not need "a palatial
stage" but may be enacted "down among the groundlings."

Accused by Claggart of mutiny and thereupon striking and
killing his accuser, Billy Budd falls like Adam, tempted (through
Eve) by the serpent; it is observed that the lifeless sergeant-at-
arms resembles "a dead snake." In the court-martial and conviction of Billy which follow, the institutionalized world has its
familiar way with the defenseless hero. But where the Hawthorne
version came to its end in the imprisonment of Donatello, a new
dimension of meaning and emotion is introduced in *Billy Budd*,
and the story moves toward ecstasy. The sense of divine command-
ment is indicated in a linking of Billy with Isaac; and the ship's
deck — where Billy lies handcuffed and at peace through the vigil
of his death — is associated with a cathedral. The pitch of exaltation is reached at the instant of the hanging.

"The last signal . . . was given. At the same moment it chanced
that the vapory fleece hanging low in the East, was shot through
with a soft glory as of the fleece of the Lamb of God seen in mystical vision and simultaneously therewith, watched by the wedged
masses of upturned faces, Billy ascended; and ascending, took the
full rose of the dawn."

After such a sentence, which is wholly saved from sentimentality
by the breath-taking detail of the "wedged masses," it must be

regretted that Melville thought it necessary to tell us that, for the sailors who witness the sacrificial death, a chip of the spar from which Billy was hanged "was as a piece of the Cross." It is enough that Captain Vere, dying himself a little time later, murmurs "Billy Budd, Billy Budd" at the last — in agony of spirit, but also in a kind of prayer. And it is enough that the manner of Billy's death transforms the sailors' mutinous anger into acceptance and understanding and that, for them, Billy is the subject of song and and fable thereafter.

Billy is the type of scapegoat hero, by whose sacrifice the sins of his world are taken away: in this case, the world of the H.M.S. "Indomitable" and the British navy, a world threatened by a mutiny which could destroy it. Melville brought to bear upon such a hero and his traditional fate an imagination of mythic capabilities: I mean an imagination able to detect the intersection of divine, supernatural power and human experience; an imagination which could suggest the theology of life without betraying the limits of literature. Hawthorne, for example, had only very faint traces of such an imagination; his fiction never (unless in *The Scarlet Letter*) rose beyond the unequivocally humanistic level of insight and expression. He realized that the "pristine virtues" would inevitably encompass their possessor's destruction; and for him the proper denouement was the acquisition through suffering of different and tougher virtues. His version of the fortunate fall found the fortune in the faller; and it suggested an acceptance of the world and its authority. In the doctrine of *felix culpa*, the Fall was regarded as fortunate not because of its effect upon Adam the sinner but because of its effect upon God the redeemer; and the world was to be transformed thereafter. Melville's achievement was to recover the higher plane of insight, without intruding God on a machine: by making the culprit himself the redeemer.

It is this, I suggest, which accounts for something that might otherwise bother us in the *novella*: the apparent absence of impressive change — not in the world but in the character of Billy Budd. We expect our tragic heroes to change and to reveal (like Donatello) a dimensionally increased understanding of man's ways or of God's ways to man. Billy is as innocent, as guileless, as trusting, as *loving*, when he hangs from the yardarm as when he is taken off the "Rights of Man." What seems like failure, in this respect and on Melville's part, is exactly the heart of the accomplishment. For the change effected in the story has to do with the *reader*, as representative of the onlooking world: with the perception forced on him of the indestructible and in some sense the absolute value of "the pristine virtues." The perception is aroused by exposing the Christ-like nature of innocence and love, which is to raise those qualities to a higher power — to their highest power. Humanly speaking, those qualities are fatal; but they alone can save the world.

So, in *Billy Budd*, Melville's own cycle of experience and commitment, which began with the hopeful dawn and "the glorious, glad, golden sun," returns again to the dawn — but a dawn transfigured, "seen in mystical vision." Melville salvaged the legend of hope both for life and for literature: by repudiating it in order to restore it in an apotheosis of its hero. There will be salvation yet, the story hints, from that treacherous dream.

Bruce R. McElderry, Jr.

From "Three Earlier Treatments of the *Billy Budd* Theme"

. . . "God bless Captain Vere!" may be, as some critics insist, the key to Melville's final philosophy,[1] but beyond question it is the essence of the popular nautical hero. *Billy Budd* has usually been discussed as if it were unique in theme, a strange, unprecedented story. Future discussion must take into account the fact that Billy Budd himself is distilled from a well-established type, the nautical hero for whom duty, no matter how unfair or unreasonable it may appear, is nevertheless the voice of God. If one recognizes this, "God bless Captain Vere!" becomes first of all what Melville said it was: "a conventional felon's benediction directed aft towards the quarters of honor. . . ."[2] It is the traditional ritual of the condemned man forgiving the official who is duty bound to order his death. Melville's achievement was to make real and convincing an attitude and a speech which for centuries has been a staple of popular accounts of executions.

From *American Literature,* XXVII (May 1955), 256-257. Reprinted by permission of Duke University Press.
[1] See, for example, F. Barron Freeman, *Melville's Billy Budd* (Cambridge, Mass., 1948), pp. 120-124.
[2] Freeman, p. 265.

William York Tindall

"The Ceremony of Innocence"

Billy Budd seems to make something almost too tidy out of what remains uncertain in *Moby Dick*. Melville's story of the captain, the villain, and the tar, apparently less a story than a commentary on one, may strike the hasty reader as a product of reason rather than imagination, as something reduced to discourse for ready apprehension by basic Englishmen. What had to be said has been said by Captain Vere or Melville himself. As critics, therefore, we may feel frustrated, as Romantics we may prefer a little teasing mystery around, and as esthetes, confronted with discourse, we are sure that talking about a thing is less admirable than embodying it in image of action. Of Kierkegaard's three categories, the esthetic, the moral, and the divine, Melville seems to have chosen the second — to the applause of some and the departure of others, for *Don Giovanni* maybe.

That the matter of *Billy Budd* gratifies what Melville calls "the moral palate" is plain from the plainest rehearsal. The scene is a

William York Tindall, "The Ceremony of Innocence (Herman Melville: *Billy Budd*)" from *Great Moral Dilemmas in Literature, Past and Present,* ed. R. M. MacIver (New York: Harper & Row, 1956), pp. 73-81. Copyright 1956 by The Institute for Religious and Social Studies. Reprinted by permission of Harper & Row, Publishers.

British frigate during the Napoleonic wars. Two mutinies have justified fears of more. Against this ominous background, Billy, an innocent aboard, is accused for no good reason by Claggart, a petty officer, of plotting mutiny. The captain, a reasonable man, doubts Claggart's story and brings Billy in to confront his lying accuser. Overcome by a stutterer's indignation, the innocent foretopman, unable to speak a word, strikes Claggart dead with a fist like a ham. Captain Vere is faced with a dilemma. Though he believes in Billy's innocence, naval law and prudence alike demand punishment for the impetuous seaman while pity and reason counsel mercy. Internal debate inclines the captain toward conviction, and Billy, condemned despite the "troubled conscience" of his judges, is hanged.

The subject is a quandary or what Melville calls "the intricacies involved in the question of moral responsibility." As the captain ponders "the moral phenomenon presented in Billy Budd" and the "elemental evil" of Claggart, he fathoms the "mystery of iniquity." The case of Billy seems, as the captain says, a matter for "psychologic theologians."

Although, as T. S. Eliot observes in *After Strange Gods*, "It is . . . during moments of moral and spiritual struggle . . . that men [in fiction] . . . come nearest being real," Billy and Claggart, who represent almost pure good and pure evil, are too simple and too extreme to satisfy the demands of realism; for character demands admixture. Their all but allegorical blackness and whiteness, however, are functional in the service of Vere's problem, and Vere, goodness knows, is real enough. Claggart is black because, as Philipp G. Frank once observed, a sinner is necessary for the realization of a moral code; and an innocent is almost equally instructive. These abstractions, a sacrifice of verismilitude to tactical necessity, reveal the "moral quality" of the captain's mind, which becomes a theater for contending opposites and eventual choice. Such dramatic crises are not only the favorite stuff of novelists but of philosophers and poets as well: Kierkegaard wrote *Either/Or* and Yeats "The Choice."

Not only rational, Vere's choice involves his whole sensitive, adult being. Agony shows on his face as he emerges from his interview with Billy, and a final exclamation shows how deeply he is stirred. Involving more than black and white, the captain's choice is between two moral codes, military and natural. The first is evident; the second is either that of the noble savage, in whom Melville was interested, or what Western culture takes for granted. In other words, the captain's conflict is between the balanced claims of justice and equity, order and confusion, law and grace, reason and feeling, or, as Melville puts it, "military duty" and "moral scruple." Vere's eloquent and moving speech to the drumhead court, the climax of such drama as there is, leaves little to add about these issues and his dilemma.

The conflict of military with natural may occupy the stage, but Melville recognizes other codes, that of custom or respectability, for example. Claggart's "natural depravity" appears in respectable guise. Melville also recognizes the cultural, psychological, and absolute bases for morality, and hints in a very modern way at their operation.

"Moral," Melville's favorite word — in this book at least — is one which, though commonly taken for granted, is slippery. I have read a thing in which "moral" means something else on every page. What Yvor Winters means by it escapes me. Vague and general like F. R. Leavis's "awareness of life" or narrow and definite like the *quid agas* of Scholastic philosophers, the word needs fixing before use. As I shall use it and as I think Melville did, morality implies not only action but motive, attitude, and being. It involves a sense of obligation to self, community, and the absolute, which provide a frame by conscience, law, tradition, or revelation. If we demand a single equivalent, Melville's "responsibility" will do.

Vere's action, however sudden and whether we approve of it or not, is plainly responsible. Billy and Claggart act, to be sure: one bears false witness and the other delivers a blow, but neither actor follows reason and each is more important for what he is than what he does. If being as well as action can be moral, however, they are moral figures, too, existing like cherubs or fiends in a moral atmosphere. Good and bad, they occupy the region of good and evil.

It is agreed by most that moral substance is necessary for the novel. Not the pure form of Flaubert's desire, and falling far short of the condition of music, the novel is an arrangement of references to vital issues, without which it is empty. A value of Joyce's *Ulysses*, for example, is the feeling and idea of charity. That moral substance fails to insure greatness, however, is proved by the works of Horatio Alger; and that it fails to guarantee moral effect is proved by those of Mickey Spillane. The errors of censors and formalists show the folly of judging by morality alone or arrangement alone. Not moral idea but its embodiment in what Eliot called objective correlatives, suitably arranged, determines value. Far from inciting action as moralizing does, embodied morality invites contemplation, and to become an object of contemplation, substance must be distanced by form. The question is not how much morality is there but how much is under control, how fully insight and moral intelligence have submitted to esthetic discipline. Our problem, then, is not morality itself but moral art or morally significant form.

Captain Vere's speech to the court adequately embodies the idea of "moral responsibility" in dramatic form; but we must find if Billy's history has found fitting embodiment. At first reading, that history seems a curious and eccentric structure of essays on ethics, digressions or "bypaths," character sketches, and chronicles of the navy, an arrangement that after uncertain progress tails inconclusively off. Such image and action as we find, failing to halt the lamentable decline, seem occasions for analysis or digression, like biblical texts in a pulpit. Since the crucial interview between Vere and Billy is disappointingly offstage, Melville seems to have avoided the dramatic possibilities of his theme. That the book calls for the dramatization he failed to give it, is proved by attempts at play and opera, which, while affirming excellence of theme, imply that action or image are better ways of presenting it. But something that continues to fascinate us in its present form and calls forth responses beyond the capacity of discourse, suggests art of another kind. Maybe Melville avoided drama in the interests of a less obvious medium.

Moby Dick assures us that Melville was an artist, not a lecturer on ethics. He not only worked three years on *Billy Budd*, but he seems to have regarded the result with far from senile favor. The first version, recently detected in manuscript by F. Barron Freeman, reveals more action and less discourse; yet this version, which corresponds more happily to what we think fiction should be, is not so effective as the one before us with all its weight of digression and analysis.

That Melville was aware of form is clear from passages in *Billy Budd*. When Captain Vere says, "With mankind forms, measured forms, are everything," he probably means usage and custom; but Melville himself, applying Vere's remark to esthetics, says that the symmetry of form desirable in pure fiction cannot be achieved in factual narrative like this. The story is not factual in fact. But Melville, wanting it to seem so, excuses apparent formlessness as a form for giving the illusion of a bare report; for truth, he continues, will always have its ragged edges and matters of fact must lack the finish of an "architectural finial." Aware of loose structure and inconclusive ending, he justifies them for what seem wrong reasons. Not reasons, however, but what he made must detain us while we scout further possibilities. The curious form he made may be functional and, for all our hasty impression and his explanation, effective. Is the book as shapeless as he implies? Or, if shapeless, is shapelessness a kind of shape? Is the book as pedestrian, discursive, and factual as he claims and as we had supposed on first looking into it?

What seems at first to be factual is presented, we find, in part by images and allusions that are incompatible with a pretense of factuality. Though unapparent, those images are livelier than we thought. Consider the coloring of the scene between decks before the execution as Billy lies in white amid profound blackness. Catching up the abstract whiteness and blackness of Billy and Claggart, this image of black and white embodies them. At the execution the rosy dawn that seems "the fleece of the Lamb of God seen in mystical vision" promises a kind of renewal while implying much else. Circling birds after the burial at sea offer by the aid of tradition some spiritual import. And that spilt soup, perhaps more action than image, carries sugestions beyond the demands of plot, suggestions so indefinite, what is more, that they confound its rational progress. Even the names of ships, though serving a more comprehensible purpose, are as significant as those in *Moby Dick*. Billy is removed from the *Rights of Man*, for instance, and Vere is mortally wounded by a shot from the *Athéiste*.

The words of *Billy Budd* carry more than denotation. "Sinister dexterity," at once witty and desolating, sounds like something from *Finnegans Wake*, where, indeed, it reappears. Vere's last words, "Billy Budd," are equivocal. Do they imply feeling, regret, self-realization, understanding? Are they a form for something incompletely realized? However "factual" the words of this pseudoreport, they function like the words of poetry.

Not only last words and indeterminate images but a number of hints about Billy's "all but feminine" nature plague our assumptions. Roses and lilies dye his cheeks. He comports himself like a "rustic beauty" at times and like a vestal virgin at others. These qualities and appearances, astonishing in an able seaman, calling forth an "ambiguous smile" from one or another of his shipmates, suggest psychological depths and motives below the level of the plain report. By virtue of such intimations Billy seems at once more and less bottomless than we had supposed, and so do the motives of Claggart, if not those of the captain himself. Among such suggestions, avoidance of the obviously dramatic becomes implicit embodiment that escapes the limits of drama.

What pleases me most, however, is the accompaniment of biblical allusions which, however unobtrusive and irregular, recurs like Wagnerian *leitmotiv*. Time and again Billy is compared to Adam and Jesus. Billy's innocence is as much that of Adam before the Fall as that of the more secular noble savage. As a "peacemaker," a term implying beatitude, Billy seems destined for "crucifixion"; and his hanging, condensing events, becomes an ascension. Vere is compared to Abraham about to sacrifice Isaac, obeying God's will with fear and trembling. Becoming a shadow of God, Vere weighs the claims of Adam and Satan. Claggart, whose denunciation is reported in Mosaic terms as "false witness," is compared not only to the Serpent of Eden but to Ananias and to one struck dead by an angel of God, "yet," as the captain says, "the angel must hang!" Man's fall and redemption and all troubles between seem suggested by this large though not fully elaborated analogy, which, bringing to mind the mythical parallels in *Ulysses* and *The Waste Land*, removes Billy a little farther from the abstraction to which, for all his stutter and those rosy cheeks, he seems committed. However incapable of supporting this mythical burden, he becomes by its aid almost as portentous as choosing Vere. The sailors, whose testimony cannot be ignored, are more impressed by Billy than by Vere, reason and all. Not only being and secular victim, Billy becomes saint and martyr and his hanging an omen. Pieces of the spar to which he quietly ascends are venerated like pieces of the true cross, suitable for reliquaries or the holiest of duffle bags. By the aid of myth and military ritual the story of Billy, transformed from an essay on good, evil, and choice, approaches what Yeats called "the ceremony of innocence."

We must conclude that Melville avoided the attractions of the obvious in the interests of indefinite suggestiveness and myth. His work, whatever its air of the factual and the discursive, is symbolist and richer for scarcity of drama and image. Such drama and images as are there function more intensely in their abstract context than profusion could. That the structure as a whole also serves esthetic purpose is likely. As we have seen, the book is a queer arrangement of discourse, action, image, and allusion, with discourse predominating. We have seen how image and action work in this mixture; but we must examine the function of discourse. In such context, discourse, increasing tension, makes allusion and image dramatic or enlarges them, and, working with allusion, image, and action may produce a third something by juxtaposition as in Eliot's *Four Quartets* or Wallace Stevens' *Notes Toward a Supreme Fiction*. Seeming now a structure of conflicts, not only of men and codes but of methods, which become a technical echo of the theme, the book emerges as a structural drama or a drama of structure. An ending that seemed weak afterthought (and was not there in the first version) now unifies all. Vere's exclamation, the saint's legend, and inconclusiveness, working together, comprise a form, which may tail off but tails suggestively off, leaving endless reverberations in our minds. There is more mystery around than we had thought, and we may agree with dying Gertrude Stein that answers are less important than questions. What at a superficial reading had the appearance of exhaustive discourse becomes inexhaustible. The shapeless thing becomes suggestive shape. Neither as loose nor as tight as it once seemed, the strange sequence of precise discourse and indefinite suggestiveness corresponds to our experience of life itself. That the form Melville made fascinates while it eludes and teases is shown no less by popular favor than by the abundance of critical comment.

However different it looks, *Billy Budd* is not altogether different in kind from *Moby Dick*, another structure of digression, discourse, action, and image. The proportions and impact may be different, the images of *Moby Dick* may be more compelling, but both serve symbolic suggestion and both are forms for offering a vision of reality. Not the tidy discourse of our first impression, the work is almost as inexplicable as *Moby Dick*.

What exactly does this form present? It is impossible to answer this question for any symbolist work; for works of this kind escape discursive accounting. We may say that *Billy Budd* is a vision of man in society, a vision of man's moral quandary or his responsibility; but its meaning is more general than these, and that is why it haunts us. So haunted, I find the work not an essay on a moral issue but a form for embodying the feeling and idea of thinking about a moral issue, the experience of facing, of choosing, of being uneasy about one's choice, of trying to know. Not a conclusion like a sermon, *Billy Budd* is a vision of confronting what confronts us, of man thinking things out with all the attendant confusions and uncertainties. Disorder is a form for this and the apparently formless book a formal triumph. To do what it does it has to be a fusion of tight-loose, shapeless-shaped, irrelevant-precise, suggestive-discursive — a mixture of myth, fact, and allusion that has values beyond reference. The discursive parts represent our attempts at

thinking, while the action, images, and allusions represent what we cannot think but must approximate. Arrangement of these discordant elements forms a picture of a process.

From my guess at meaning it follows that the center of this form is neither Vere nor Billy but rather the teller of the story or Melville himself. Though ghostlier, he is not unlike the Marlow of Conrad's *Lord Jim* and *Heart of Darkness* or the Quentin of Faulkner's *Absalom, Absalom!* Using Vere and Billy as materials, Melville's thought-process, like those of Marlow and Quentin, is the heart of this darkness and its shape the objective correlative, a form for something at once imperfectly understood and demanding understanding. Morality, the substance of this form, becomes an element that limits and directs the feelings and ideas created by the whole. Moral substance, what is more, may be what engages our minds while the form does its work. Value, not from morality alone, issues from the form that includes it and in which it serves. If the form concerned less, I repeat, it would be trivial, but without its formal presentation the morality would remain in Sunday school.

United now, the beautiful and the good create a vision larger than either, a vision transcending the case of Billy Budd or the quandary of Captain Vere. The teller, now any man, presents man's feeling in the face of any great dilemma. Thought and feeling, outdistancing themselves, become objects of contemplation, remote yet immediate. The effect of this form is moral in the sense of enlarging our awareness of human conditions or relationships and of improving our sensitivity. In such a form Kierkegaard's esthetic, moral, and divine become a single thing.

Harry Levin

From *The Power of Blackness*

The Confidence-Man, which marks the nadir of his confidence in society and nature, and in himself as well, is the terminus of authorship for Melville. His additional narrative, *Billy Budd,* which would be begun a full generation later and not quite finished at his death, should therefore stand apart from the main body of his work. Its deferred publication in our time, together with its sentimental appeal to some critics, may have disproportionately affected our understanding of Melville in his totality. Though it adds an impressive last word to many of his longstanding preoccupations, it is unevenly written, and would seem to be more of a postscript than a testament. Its point of departure is a retrospective dedication to Jack Chase, the ideal British shipmate of *White-Jacket.* But if he is more youthfully reincarnate in the blond and blue-eyed Billy Budd, the angle of vision has changed; the writer is not a budding seaman looking up to an elder comrade, but an old man who has lost both his sons, one of them apparently by suicide. On the other hand, after the arbitrary despotism of Melville's earlier

From Harry Levin, *The Power of Blackness* (New York: Alfred A. Knopf, 1958), pp. 195-197. © Copyright 1958 by Harry Levin. Reprinted by permission of Alfred A. Knopf, Inc.

78

captains, the commanding officer under whom his protagonist now serves, "starry Vere," treats him with fatherly — not to say godly — consideration. The story takes its politico-historical bearings from certain mutinies in the British Navy during the epoch of the French Revolution; it also echoes a nearer controversy in the United States Navy, where one of Melville's cousins sat on the court-martial. But Melville broadens, even more than usual, the parable of naval discipline. His "inside story" of the boyish civilian, impressed from the merchantman, the Rights of Man, to the man-of-war, H.M.S. Indomitable, is a *mysterium iniquitatis*, another inquiry into the problem of evil, as charted against the intersecting lines of free will and necessity.

On the assumption that "the physical make" is in keeping with "the moral nature," a fair exterior is again conventionally equated with goodness, and it is assumed that "the Handsome Sailor" will behave handsomely. But Melville instances the birthmark in Hawthorne's tale to indicate the flaw that so pointedly qualifies Billy's perfection: a stammer, a hesitation of speech, a mental articulation which lags behind his muscular reflexes. Toward him the jet-curled Claggart, master-at-arms, feels an antipathy which might have been sympathy, an animus which is clearly attributable to a frustrated homosexual impulse, though it is set forth as an ethical contrast rather than as a psychological motive. When the angelic Billy is traduced by his diabolical foe, he cannot speak; he is unable to comprehend the malevolence that could bear false witness against him. In his bewilderment, he strikes out, and Claggart is struck dead. If this act is not physically improbable, it is morally indefensible; yet Melville lays it down as the condition of his dilemma. Billy has been "a sort of upright barbarian," like Hawthorne's Donatello; he has shown the primitivistic simplicity of "a period prior to Cain's city and citified man," not unlike Melville's South Sea islanders. He is a specimen of mankind, Melville tells us, "who in the nude might have posed for a statue of young Adam before the fall." If we follow the parallel, we infer that the original sin was to strike back in revenge against dire provocation; hence Billy too, no less than the Negro slaves rebelling against Benito Cereno, no less than the Indian-hater resorting to force in *The Confidence-Man*, is a revenger. And the good man, as Pierre learned from *Hamlet*, has no retaliation which will keep his goodness intact; he cannot fight the world's evils without becoming entrammeled in them himself; whether he resists or suffers them, he is overwhelmed.

This may help to explain the paradox that Hawthorne's protagonists come to grief when they ignore the heart, while Melville's
do when they make it their sole guide. The heart, with its feminine
sensibilities, will always be on Billy's side, as Captain Vere
acknowledges in his compunctious summation of the case; and so
will nature, whose primeval element is the ocean. But manhood, on
joining the navy, submits itself to the King's law; and whether we
take that as the naval code or the divine order, its decree is that
"the angel must hang." Here, at last, there is no ambiguity between the celestial and the terrestrial. Ishmael may waver between
Plato's *Phaedo* and Bowditch's *Practical Navigator;* but Socrates
himself, when he was condemned by the Athenians, bowed to their
condemnation. More concerned with the apologue than the psychology, Melville draws a curtain over the farewell interview between Billy and Captain Vere; their relation has been prefigured
in that of Isaac and Abraham, and commented upon in Kirke-
gaard's *Fear and Trembling;* yet the filial sacrifice, averted in the
Old Testament, must be consummated here. The accident of
White-Jacket's fall from the mast becomes a ritual with Billy's
execution — and Melville purifies it by carefully affirming that it
is not accompanied, as hangings usually are, with a sexual spasm.
Jumping from the yard-arm with the shout, "God bless Captain
Vere!", Billy accepts the justice of the sentence.* Does Melville? He
could not have gone on existing for so long unless, with Margaret
Fuller's sweeping concession, he had accepted the universe. But that
acceptance, whole-hearted at the beginning, was subjected increasingly to re-examination. The alternative of rejection has its em-
phatic counterstatement in *The Confidence-Man;* and, though it
may be finally neutralized in *Billy Budd,* the outcome seems at
best to be a truce.

---

* [Actually, Billy does not jump from the yard-arm, but is hauled up to it.—
EDITOR.]

Richard Harter Fogle

From *"Billy Budd*: The Order of the Fall"

Billy Budd is a tragedy, in that it presents an action of great magnitude which develops a dilemma insoluble without loss of one good in the preservation or achievement of another. Or, in other words, two different and irreconcilable systems, in this instance the order of nature and the order of the British Navy, clash directly. Captain Vere is forced to choose the order of the Navy and therefore sacrifice the innocent Billy Budd, the natural man. We sympathize with Vere, but such is the complexity of the considerations involved that we are not quite sure that he has chosen rightly; there are some grounds for arguing that the sacrifice of Billy was avoidable. There is a tragic reconciliation, however, for the memory of Billy lives on as a Christ of the sailors, as a bright spot of meaning and hope against a dark background. His kingdom is not of this world, but it exists. *Billy Budd* is tragedy, too, in providing the increase of knowledge that we have rightly come to attach to tragedy. The confrontation of opposing characters in crucial action, if properly conducted, enlarges our knowledge of the potentialities

© 1960 by The Regents of the University of California. Reprinted from *Nineteenth-Century Fiction*, xv, No. 3 (December 1960), 190-191, by permission of The Regents.

of human nature and of the circumstances under which human beings exist. Perhaps it should be added, through in any event no exact alignment is being attempted here, that *Billy Budd* differs from classical tragedy in introducing positive and fundamental evil as the immediate cause of the catastrophe in the person of the master-at-arms, Claggart. Without this irrational and inexplicable element of evil, which functions as chance, the order of nature and the order of the Navy under the Mutiny Act might have lived together without an open breach.

Walter Sutton

"Melville and the Great
God Budd"

The vogue of Zen Buddhism among such writers as J. D. Salinger
in the East and the San Francisco Bohemians is nothing new on
the American scene. The attachment of these writers to Eastern
mysticism links them with the Romantics of the nineteenth century, and the impulse in both periods reveals a desire for certainty,
or at least a point of rest, in a confused and rapidly-changing
world. In an earlier day Emerson, the Transcendentalist preacher
who could not hold to a Christian creed, was attracted to the
sacred books of India. Thoreau at Walden pondered the *Bhagavad-
Gita* with the whistle of the steam locomotive, the improved means
to an unimproved end, in his ears. Whitman, with whom the
"Beat" writers most consciously identify, attempted to relate the
technology of his day to the mystical heritage of the East.

But rather than these Romantics, who were idealists and cosmic
optimists, it is their contemporary, Herman Melville, writing in a
later day, who stands closest to our time because of his pessimism
and his interest in Buddhist thought specifically. A poem entitled

"Buddha," extolling the state of Nirvana, appeared in *Timoleon*, the volume of poems published in 1891, the year of his death. "Rammon," an uncompleted sketch preserved with his unpublished poetry, has as its title character a royal disciple of Buddha. But the most important and relevant work is the short novel *Billy Budd*, like *Timoleon* completed in the closing months of his life.

It has been suggested that Melville's interest in Buddhism dates from his journey to the Mediterranean countries and the Near East in the dark winter of 1857-58, when his career as a novelist was ending. A more immediate source of inspiration can be found in the pessimistic philosophy of Arthur Schopenhauer in which Melville steeped himself during the last years of his life. Merton Sealts' checklist of Melville's reading indicates that he owned and marked an 1888 edition of *The World as Will and Idea*, translated by Haldane and Kemp. He also read T. Bailey Saunders' translation of separate volumes of the essays — including *Counsels and Maxims, Religion, Studies in Pessimism*, and *The Wisdom of Life* — during 1890 and 1891, the period of composition of *Billy Budd* and of some of the *Timoleon* poems. For Schopenhauer, as both *The World as Will and Idea* and the essays attest, Buddhism was the most enlightened of religions. The concepts of Buddhism, as interpreted by Schopenhauer, were particularly congenial to Melville during his last years. They help to explain some of the problems of motivation in *Billy Budd* and to make possible a consistent reading of the work.

It has been debated whether the story of the handsome young sailor with the attributes of both Adam and Christ should be read as a "testament of acceptance," a mellow reconciliation with an ultimately-benign Providence, or as a bitter, if understated, final protest against an unjust God or an unjust world in which an unjust God has no business not existing. Melville's attitude in his earlier novels is hardly a model of acceptance or resignation. Although even as early as his first novel, *Typee* (1846), we see in his hero a motive toward negation and withdrawal, it is habitually balanced by an assertion of the will to live and to realize positive values. In the early works, at least through *Moby Dick* (1851), the conflict between these two motives is a major tension.

However, beginning with *Pierre* (1852) and carrying through to the close of Melville's brief career as a novelist with the publication of *The Confidence-Man* in 1857, there is evidence of a deepening disillusion that is in keeping with Schopenhauer's emphasis, supported by Buddhism (just as Emersonian Transcendentalism was supported by Hindu mysticism), upon the meaninglessness of the phenomenal world. In the story "Bartleby," first published in 1853, we find a hero who, in instinctive revulsion from his world of experience, has conquered his will to live and achieved the complete withdrawal of the hunger artist. In Buddhist terms, this is Nirvana, extinction, or nothingness, the ultimate antithesis to an existence of pain and suffering. Although the tone of this quiet story is bitter, the point of view of the author is close to that of the closing years of his life, when, still pondering the conflict of convictions that animates his earliest and most spontaneous work, he found solace in Schopenhauer's philosophy of negation. The acknowledged affinities of this philosophy with Buddhism can help us understand *Billy Budd,* Melville's beautifully-constructed novella.

In this story there is a deliberately-maintained balance between a naturalistic and a providential or redemptive view of the fate of the victim-hero Billy. Although the hanging of the young Adam-Christ is described in religious terms (Billy, "ascending, took the full rose of the dawn"), his inert lifelessness is also emphasized, and his ascension is mechanical and abortive, limited as it is to the height of the ship's yardarm. While criticism generally has tended to emphasize *either* the naturalistic *or* the Christian-redemptive interpretation, there has been less regard for a controlling perspective from which both of these interpretations of Billy's fate, or of human existence, are regarded as equally illusory.

In this view, reinforced for Melville by Schopenhauer's discussion of Buddhism, life is a painful experience beset by four evils: birth, age, sickness, and death. Nirvana, the state in which these four *things* no longer exist, is the consummation of life. In Melville's poem "Buddha," published in 1891, the appeal of the release offered by the Buddhist ideal is directly expressed:

> Swooning swim to less and less,
>   Aspirant to nothingness!
> Sobs of the worlds, and dole of kinds
>   That dumb endurers be—
> Nirvana! absorb us in your skies,
>   Annul us into thee.

The desire for a release from a life of suffering is regarded as universal by Schopenhauer. In *The World as Will and Idea,* he describes the "knowledge that we had better not be" as "the most important of all truths." If we acknowledge the existence of this intellectual "truth," for the purpose of reading *Billy Budd* at least (it is implicitly endorsed by Melville's poem), some of the difficulties in understanding the motivation of the character of Captain Vere are removed. If we attribute to Vere (*veritas*) an apprehension of this "truth," we can understand more easily his feverish zeal to condemn Billy to death summarily at the drumhead court-martial — a zeal regarded as unnatural by the subordinate officers of the court, who are inclined to credit the extenuating circumstances involved in Billy's killing of Claggart, the master-at-arms who had falsely accused him of mutinous acts. From Vere's point of view, however, the avoidance of prolonged suffering and the immediate execution of the innocent youth who has run afoul of a merciless law can be understood to be less a punishment than a boon.

Now the captain, known as "Starry Vere," is characterized not only as a contemplative and thoughtful man but also as a man of "settled convictions," which stood "as a dyke against those invading waters of novel opinion social political and otherwise, which carried away as in a torrent no few minds in those days, minds by nature not inferior to his own." As an aristocrat Vere opposes revolutionary innovations disinterestedly, not because of his stake in society, but because the revolutionary ideals seem "incapable of embodiment in lasting institutions." In such a conservative, sensitive to the need for order, one might expect a wholehearted commitment to the law, which Billy has transgressed. Yet such is not the case. In the trial scene Vere asserts the existence of two laws: the civil code — represented by the Articles of War — by which Vere and the members of the court are bound as officers, and the law of nature — romantically identified with the heart — in the light of which Billy is innocent. By suggesting the primacy of the law of the heart while at the same time accepting the destructive law which must be enforced, Vere implicitly acknowledges the bankruptcy of his romantic idealism. His asertion of the claims of both laws shows the captain to be a relativist, although he cannot be satisfied with anything short of absolutism. The situation of a character who, longing for certainty, is inexorably caught in a relativistic world is the classic predicament of the hero of Melville's later works, from the time of *Pierre* (1852). It is also a predicament which makes its victim ripe for an absolutist point of view from which all human laws and values are seen as illusions.

At any event, Billy himself — after his closeted interview with Vere, who communicates the sentence of the court—is represented as completely resigned to his fate. The "tension of his agony" is over, having been resolved by "something healing" in his talk with Vere. With the rope around his neck, Billy faces death with equanimity, almost cheerfully, in keeping with his habitual good nature. His unexpected valediction — "God bless Captain Vere!" — comes from his lips like "the clear melody of a singing-bird on the point of launching from the twig." Schopenhauer, at the close of his chapter on death in *The World as Will and Idea*, remarks that "to die willingly, to die joyfully, is the prerogative of the resigned, of him who surrenders and denies the will to live." For Billy, the conquest of the will to live seems complete, especially in view of the strange circumstance that no struggle or convulsive movement is apparent in the hanging, as his pinioned figure arrives at the yard end, with no motion, says Melville in a beautifully-cadenced line, "save that created by the slow roll of the hull, in moderate weather so majestic in a great ship heavy-cannoned."

This strange bodily quiescence — suggestive of a mental acceptance of death — prompts the superstitious purser to propose to the unreceptive surgeon, the apostle of science, that the manner of Billy's death is a "testimony to the force lodged in will-power" and a "species of euthanasia" rather than an actual death by hanging. The term *euthanasia* is interesting, because the same word is equated by Schopenhauer with the Buddhist term *Nirvana*. In his *Counsels and Maxims* he describes euthanasia as "an easy death, not ushered in by disease, and free from all pain and struggle." For Schopenhauer, as for the Buddhist, death in this form is not an evil but the highest consummation of life.

The reunuciation of the will achieved by Billy is not attained by the captain. As observed after his interview with Billy, his face is expressive of a suffering greater than that of the condemned victim. It is clear that Captain Vere is still living in the agony of the will. Yet it seems that Vere recognizes in Billy an ideal of renunciation toward which he aspires, although he is fated to maintain the role of a responsible and guilty actor in a painful world.

That the image of Billy remains such an ideal is suggested by the manner of Vere's death. After having received a fatal wound in battle, he lies in a Gibraltar hospital "under the influence of that magical drug which, soothing the physical frame, mysteriously operates on the subtler element in man." While in this condition, shortly before his death, Vere is heard to repeat, not in "accents of remorse," the name of Billy Budd. At this point, Vere's state reminds one of Melville's lines ("Swooning swim to less and less,/

Aspirant to nothingness"), and the name of Billy Budd, which he utters prayerfully, may be identified in his mind with the ideal of renunciation — a renunciation which, in the form of Nirvana, or a final release, Vere himself is at last about to experience.

One Buddhist concept is central in Melville's controlling point of view in this last completed novel. This is the idea, as rendered by Schopenhauer in *The World as Will and Idea*, that "in the world all is illusion, there is no reality in the thing; all is empty." This attitude also applies to religious beliefs. Schopenhauer cites Shakespeare and Goethe as examples of genius who rise above all conventional beliefs and who cannot be conceived of as spokesmen for any religious orthodoxy.

From this perspective, to which Melville was no stranger even as early as *The Confidence-Man* (1857), there is no Great God Budd. The idol, the presented image, the rationalized god of any religious creed is simply an illusion of the limited, conventional mind. The image has meaning only as an outward symbol of an inner state. Buddhism is not concerned with the concept of God, which it neither affirms nor denies. It is concerned with the attainment of an inner reality which it describes variously as Nirvana, or emptiness, or *nothing*.

The state of nothingness was a concern of Melville even in his earlier work. It was the abyss suspected behind the whiteness of the whale, imaged as the "Descartian vortices" over which we hover in conscious existence. The apprehension of this nothingness was valued by Melville as a mark of poetic insight. It was the "blackness" that he admired in Hawthorne. It was the final wisdom — "that which we seek and shun" — at Shakespeare's core.

The theme of nothingness, which Melville in his earlier work treated with mingled awe and revulsion, is developed in *Billy Budd* in a different spirit — one that is harmonious with the ideal of acceptance and renunciation in Buddhism which teaches, in Schopenhauer's words, the desirability of nonbeing as "the most important of all truths." In the face of this "truth," the objective world of things and human ideas of divine providence are alike meaningless. This view can help us appreciate the detachment and impartiality with which Melville developed his counterpoised naturalistic and Christian-redemptive frames of reference for the archetypal story of his sacrificial victim hero. From the perspective of ultimate withdrawal, both of these opposed patterns of rationalization of the human predicament — the rational-scientific and the conventionally-religious — seem twin chimeras of what Melville describes as "this incongruous world of ours" in a cancelled note to his original manuscript of the story.

The Buddhist idea of the illusory nature of human existence is integral to Melville's final point of view. The epigraph of his poem "Buddha" reads, "For what is your life? It is even as a vapor that appeareth for a little time and then vanisheth away." This relegation of human life and man's rationalizations of it to the realm of illusion serves as a kind of synthesis of the antitheses of nay and yea with which Melville had striven during most of his career. For Melville at this period — as for numerous writers of our own time, conditioned by Existentialism — the Buddhist ideal of *nothingness* seems to have been a welcome alternative to a painful and uncertain existence. His final detachment — pessimistic though it was — proved an advantage in the writing of *Billy Budd* because it enabled him to develop the dramatic conflict of skepticism and faith, of a naturalistic as against a religious view of life, with surer control and more successful form than in any of his earlier novels.

Merlin Bowen

From *The Long Encounter*

. . . There has been for many years a tendency to see in *Billy Budd* Melville's last "testament of acceptance," his long-delayed recognition of necessity — almost, as it were, the deathbed recantation of his "absolutist" errors: the author becomes his own chastened Babbalanja, kneeling on the Serenian sands to beg forgiveness for his past impiety and madness. (One wonders here to what extent this judgment may rest upon a too unqualified identification of Melville with the more intransigent of his heroes.) In such a view, at any rate, Captain Vere commonly assumes the stature of a tragic hero. He is seen as a brooding and compassionate Lincoln, courageously facing up to the hard necessities of action and responsibility, as a sort of latter-day Abraham "resolutely offering [young Isaac] up in obedience to the exacting behest."[1] What somehow goes unnoticed is that the action of hanging Billy is undertaken in clear opposition to Vere's own conscience and in obedience to "the exacting behest" not of God but of social expediency.

From *The Long Encounter: Self and Experience in the Writings of Herman Melville* (Chicago: University of Chicago Press, 1960), pp. 216-233. Reprinted by permission of The University of Chicago Press. © 1960 by The University of Chicago.
[1] *Billy Budd,* in *The Portable Melville,* p. 720.

There are, it is true, several considerations that would seem to invite such an interpretation: the circumstances of the work's composition, so like those of that other supposed farewell to life, Shakespeare's *Tempest;* the quiet, unrhetorical, and "reasonable" character of the style; the frequently eqivocal nature of the narrator's comments; and, finally, one may guess, the experience of our own generation with a like crisis of civilization so immense as to dwindle, as it seems, all merely personal values and standards.

Surely, though, it must come as a shock to any reader of Melville to find him here at the end of a long and deeply considered life with nothing more to show for it than this sorry wisdom of resignation to a forced complicity in evil. Nothing in the earlier writings— certainly not in *Clarel* — could have led one to predict so complete a reversal of attitude. And when one remembers the motto — "Keep true to the dreams of thy youth" — glued to the inside of the writing box on which *Billy Budd* was composed, one's doubts of such an interpretation grow.

Fortunately, there is no need to rely upon external probabilities in disputing such a view. The pages of *Billy Budd* themselves contain sufficient evidence upon which to base a quite different estimate of Captain Vere. According to this view, he appears as a uniformed and conscientious servant of "Cain's city," an over-civilized man who has stifled the sound of his own heart and learned to live by the head alone as his calling requires, who has abdicated his full humanity in the interests of a utilitarian social ethic and postponed the realization of truth and justice to some other and more convenient world. Neither the Christian gospel nor the modern doctrine of the rights of man has, in his opinion, any place in the government of his man-of-war world. And when the simple and loyal-hearted sailor, Billy Budd, left speechless by Claggart's accusation of treason, impulsively knocks the liar down and so kills him, the practical Vere knows his duty at once and resolutely proceeds to hang, for the greatest good of the greatest number, a man innocent in all but the most technical sense of the word.

To state the facts thus baldly is to express perhaps too harsh a judgment. One must admit that there is something deeply pathetic in the spectacle of a man fundamentally good, as Vere is, being led by the logic of his assumptions into so false a dilemma and so fatal a resolution. But to go beyond pity, as some critics do, and to discover in his collaboration with admitted evil the elements of heroism or philosophic wisdom is surely to infer beyond the presented evidence and to slide over the book's many indications of Vere's narrowness and rigidity. *Billy Budd* will appear as a much more coherent, though still puzzling, work of art if regarded as a study in the possible consequences of a commitment to a fixed and theoretic pattern rather than to patternless life itself with all its contradictions, crosscurrents, and inescapable risks.

In the book's central opposition of civilization and nature, head and heart, there can be no real question where Captain the Honorable Edward Fairfax Vere stands: quite clearly, and despite his own instinctive feelings in the matter,[2] he stands with Claggart and against Billy. By both temperament and training, he is much closer to the petty officer he despises than to the young foretopman he admires. There does exist, of course, an obvious difference of intention (or wish) between the two officers; but this difference remains, by Vere's insistence that "private conscience" must not oppose the naval code, a purely theoretical one, with no slightest influence upon conduct, and for this reason it can hardly be called a moral difference at all.

Captain Vere's political faith is here very much to the point. As he is described to us, he appears as a Burkean conservative of the strictest sort, whose faith lies neither in man nor in "novel opinions" but in proved and "lasting institutions."[3] Billy, it will be recalled, has been forcibly impressed into the service of these institutions from aboard the merchantman "Rights-of-Man," named for Thomas Paine's famous "rejoinder to Burke's arraignment of the French Revolution."[4] Recent disorders in France and even within the British navy itself have seriously alarmed Vere. Distrustful of his own men,[5] he has even less confidence in the general mass: " 'With mankind' he would say 'forms, measured forms, are everything; and that is the import couched in the story of Orpheus with his lyre spell-binding the wild denizens of the wood.' And this he once applied to the disruption of forms going on across the Channel and the consequences thereof."[6] Nature has for him the connotation of disorder, and he fears it accordingly. When, anxious for an immediate conviction of Billy and alarmed by what he considers the "scruples" of his court, he reminds his officers that " 'our allegiance is [not] to Nature [but] to the King,' " he is not

---

[2] *Ibid.*, pp. 693, 696-97.
[3] *Ibid.*, pp. 660-66.
[4] *Ibid.*, pp. 644-45.
[5] *Ibid.*, pp. 698-99, 707, 717-18.
[6] *Ibid.*, p. 734.

speaking metaphorically: the king he has in mind is George III, and he is calling upon his officers to reject the natural in favor, not of the supernatural, but of the artificial, in the form of a particular, imperfect social order. They have in fact, he reminds them, already made that choice, for

> "in receiving our commissions we in the most important regards ceased to be natural free agents. When war is declared, are we the commissioned fighters previously consulted? We fight at command. If our judgments approve the war, that is but coincidence. . . . So now. For suppose condemnation to follow these present proceedings. Would it be so much we ourselves that would condemn as it would be martial law operating through us? For that law and the rigor of it, we are not responsible. Our vowed responsibility is in this: That however pitilessly that law may operate in any instance, we nevertheless adhere to it and administer it."[7]

Billy, on the other hand, has participated in no such compact, has signed away nothing. Born outside the law as a natural child, he remains "little more than a sort of upright barbarian, much . . . as Adam presumably might have been ere the urbane Serpent wriggled himself into his company." He wears, it is true, though not by choice, "the external uniform of civilization," but this is a matter of the surface only: his peculiar virtues, "pristine and unadulterate," derive "from a period prior to Cain's city and citified man."[8] Yet, he is no anarchist. His loyalty is no less true than Vere's, but it is a simpler and far less abstract thing — essentially a sort of heartfelt personal gratitude and love: " 'I have eaten the King's bread and I am true to the King.' "[9] Such a sentiment has much less to recommend it to the "thoroughly civilized" mind than has the "austere patriotism" of Claggart[10] — so serviceable to authority, so zealous for order, so irrespective of persons. And where artificial virtues are thus honored above the natural, evil is certain to prosper: "Civilization, especially if of the austerer sort, is auspicious to it. It folds itself in the mantle of respectability."[11] Each finds that it can make use of the other. A sense, upon a prior occasion, of something "superserviceable and strained" about Claggart's zeal has not led Vere to dispense with the informer's services. And

---

[7] *Ibid.*, pp. 714-15.
[8] *Ibid.*, pp. 647-49; see also p. 696.
[9] *Ibid.*, p. 709.
[10] *Ibid.*, p. 666.
[11] *Ibid.*, pp. 674-75.

in the end it is through Vere that Claggart's wish for Billy's destruction is accomplished, and by Vere's refusal to publish the truth that the lie of Claggart's fidelity and Billy's depravity gains acceptance as the authorized account.

Vere's excessive intellectuality is a second consideration aligning him with his despised but useful master-at-arms. The simple and unsophisticated Billy is an illiterate, endowed only with "that kind and degree of intelligence going along with the unconventional rectitude of a sound human creature, one to whom not yet has been proffered the questionable apple of knowledge."[12] But Claggart's "general aspect and manner" hint of an education quite above the demands of his office, and "his brow [is] of the sort phrenologically associated with more than average intellect."[13] (It is upon·this forehead, "so shapely and intellectual-looking a feature in the master-at-arms," that Billy's fatal blow is later to fall.)[14] Billy's face, on the other hand, is "without the intellectual look of the pallid Claggart's, [but] none the less [is] it lit, like his, from within, though from a different source. The bonfire in his heart [makes] luminous the rose-tan in his cheek."[15]

Lacking as he is in any qualities that might be called brilliant,[16] Captain Vere is one of those who live by the head. His "philosophical austerity"[17] leaves little room for feeling. Exhibiting "a marked leaning toward everything intellectual," he reads much and thoughtfully, if within a rather narrow range, preferring those books which treat of "actual men and events" — the world as it is — to those which address the imagination.[18] These "unshared studies [,] modifying and tempering the practical training of an active career," have the effect of making him seem to certain of his fellow officers somewhat "pedantic" and remote from life — "a dry and bookish gentleman."[19] "A certain dreaminess of mood" comes over him at times which, when unavoidably broken in upon by a subordinate, may be transformed into a flash of unexpected but instantly controlled anger. Control is perhaps his most marked characteristic. Habitually grave in his bearing, he has "little appreciation of mere humor," and is by rigorous training, if not by

[12] *Ibid.*, pp. 648-49.
[13] *Ibid.*, p. 662.
[14] *Ibid.*, p. 702.
[15] *Ibid.*, p. 677.
[16] *Ibid.*, p. 659.
[17] *Ibid.*, p. 736.
[18] *Ibid.*, p. 660.
[19] *Ibid.*, p. 661.

nature, "the most undemonstrative of men."[20] His is "a mind resolute to surmount difficulties even if against primitive instincts strong as the wind and the sea."[21] The problem which Billy's impulsive act has placed before the court appears to him a practical one to be settled on purely rational grounds. Fearful of the still insufficiently "formalized humanity" of his officers, he warns them not to admit the heart to their councils:

> "But the exceptional in the matter moves the hearts within you. Even so too is mine moved. But let not warm hearts betray heads that should be cool. Ashore in a criminal case will an upright judge allow himself off the bench to be waylaid by some tender kinswoman of the accused seeking to touch him with her tearful plea? Well the heart, sometimes the feminine in man, here is as that piteous woman, and hard though it be, she must here be ruled out."[22]

The officers, less intellectually agile than he, seem not to notice the flaw in his analogy — at any rate do not venture to point out that what the heart asks in this case is not gratuitous mercy but ordinary justice, which is never disregardful of intent. But they remain "less convinced than agitated by the course of [his] argument."[23] When, finally, they do yield, it is not because their "scruples" have been dissipated but because they have been overawed by Vere's superior mind and crowded into action by his representations of urgency.[24] They have been given, too, their captain's personal assurance that he sympathizes with his victim as deeply as they; and in that knowledge there is perhaps some comfort for them, if no help for Billy. " 'Budd's intent or non-intent [Vere has earlier instructed them] is nothing to the purpose' "; their concern must be with his deed alone.[25] Fortunately, it is quite otherwise with the judges' act: here it is the intent and not the deed that matters. " 'I feel as you do for this unfortunate boy [Vere assures them]. But did he know our hearts, I take him to be of that generous nature that he would feel even for us on whom in this military necessity so heavy a compulsion is laid.' "[26]

The nature of that alleged compulsion deserves a more careful

---

[20] *Ibid.*, pp. 658-59.
[21] *Ibid.*, p. 713.
[22] *Ibid.*, p. 715.
[23] *Ibid.*
[24] *Ibid.*, pp. 717-18.
[25] *Ibid.*, p. 716.
[26] *Ibid.*, p. 717.

examination. Vere, is, to begin with, no simple impressed seaman but an officer and therefore a volunteer. He is also, as Melville is at some pains to emphasize, a mature, thoughtful, and morally sensitive man who presumably knew what he was doing when he accepted his commission and so placed himself in the service of a military code whose brutishness he abhors.[27] If, as he now intimates, his buttons and epaulets were purchased at the cost of his independence as a moral being, it must be admitted that the bargain was his own. His reason for making it seems clear enough from the evidence furnished us: he is deeply, indeed fanatically, committed to the maintenance of the established order as the sole means of preserving "the peace of the world and the true welfare of mankind."[28] And as the happiness of the human species seems to him dependent upon "lasting institutions," so these in turn rest upon the disciplined strength of the British fleet, "the right arm of a Power then all but the sole free conservative one of the Old World."[29] With so clear a view of the steps leading to "the true welfare of mankind," it is not surprising that in what seems to him a grave emergency Vere should dismiss the voice of conscience as an irrelevance,[30] relegate the whole question of moral intent to the leisured speculations of casuists and "psychologic theologians," and resign himself with an almost Plinlimmonish acquiescence to the unattainability of true justice this side of " 'the Last Assizes.' "[31]

Clearly, it is for this world that Captain Vere's most anxious cares are felt. The interests of the next world are represented locally by the chaplain, and the captain is no doubt happy to reciprocate that gentleman's religious care not to over-step the limits of his jurisdiction.[32] Like every sensible commander, he takes the navy as he finds it, accepting philosophically such established evils as impressment, spying, and flogging.[33] He conducts the business of his ship strictly according to China time; and if God chooses to send one of His Greenwich chronometers aboard, He does so at His own risk. " 'Struck dead by an angel of God,' " Vere exclaims as he looks down at the fallen Claggart. " 'Yet the angel must hang!' "[34] One is reminded of the answer of another practical man

27 *Ibid.*, p. 716.
28 *Ibid.*, pp. 660-61, 734.
29 *Ibid.*, p. 651.
30 *Ibid.*, pp. 715-16.
31 *Ibid.*, pp. 711-12, 714, 716.
32 *Ibid.*, p. 727.
33 *Ibid.*, pp. 696-97, 666, 695, 666-67.
34 *Ibid.*, p. 703.

in an earlier book when begged to intercede for the life of a boy condemned to death for a cause of conscience: " 'Speak not,' said Media. 'His fate is fixed. Let [the world] stand.' "[35]

But one must be careful — as Melville himself is — not to make a monster of Vere. He is neither a sadist nor a conscious hypocrite. If he is cruel, if he is sometimes not wholly honest with himself and others, these faults are rather the consequences of a principled expediency and an excessive caution.

Caution is, of course, constitutional with him. As the rule of the heart declares itself in an impulsiveness bordering at times on rashness, so the rule of the head is commonly evidenced by a habit of guarded circumspection. Claggart, for instance, is gifted with "an uncommon prudence" and brings to the accomplishment of his irrational aim "a cool judgment[,] sagacious and sound."[36] And Captain Vere, on his part, would seem to be the very soul of caution. Of his personal courage, of course, there can be no serious question: that has already been proved in a number of naval engagements.[37] But where the safety of his ship — and, by extension, of the fleet and civilization — seems to him concerned, he becomes suspicious and fearful in the extreme.

The master-at-arms, it appears, knows this trait of his captain well enough and plays upon it adroitly — almost too adroitly, since he arouses his anger — when giving "evidence" against Billy at the mainmast.[38] Vere impatiently brushes aside the imputation of fear on his part; but the seed has been planted with Iago-like cunning and almost immediately begins to put forth shoots. Fearfulness certainly lies behind Vere's strange decision to test the informer's truthfulness by a private confrontation with the accused rather than by a formal examination of witnesses.[39] What legally admissible evidence he could hope to obtain by such a confrontation is not at all clear, but what does in point of fact happen is that he himself thereby sets up the fatal situation and invites disaster. The point was not lost upon that "self-poised character of . . . grave sense and experience," the ship's surgeon. Leaving Vere's cabin under a strict injunction of secrecy after certifying the death of the master-at-arms,

---

[35] *Mardi,* II, 30 (chap. cxii).
[36] *Billy Budd,* in *The Portable Melville,* pp. 680, 675.
[37] *Ibid.,* pp. 657-58.
[38] *Ibid.,* pp. 695-96.
[39] *Ibid.,* pp. 698-99.

he could not help thinking how more than futile the utmost discretion sometimes proves in this human sphere, subject as it is to unforseeable fatalities; the prudent method adopted by Captain Vere to obviate publicity and trouble having resulted in an event that necessitated the former, and, under existing circumstances in the navy, indefinitely magnified the latter.[40]

And with Claggart now dead at Billy's hand, the same spirit of fearfulness dictates the secrecy and precipitation of Vere's action in calling a drumhead court-martial: "Feeling that unless quick action were taken on it, the deed of the Foretopman, so soon as it should be known on the gun-decks, would tend to awaken any slumbering embers of the Nore [Mutiny] among the crew, a sense of the urgency of the case overruled in Captain Vere every other consideration."[41] Justice, clearly, is such a consideration. He has known from the first that " 'the angel must hang,' "[42] and in the light of this prejudgment of the case the body he convokes appears less a court of law than a convenient instrument of his will.

A not entirely disinterested prudence, the narrator hints, underlies Vere's decision to proceed against Billy by court-martial rather than by the open exercise of those summary powers legally his as captain:

. . . though a conscientious disciplinarian he was no lover of authority for mere authority's sake. Very far was he from embracing opportunities for monopolizing to himself the perils of moral responsibility — none at least that could properly be referred to an official superior or shared with him by his official equals or even subordinates. So thinking, he was glad it would not be at variance with usage to turn the matter over to a summary court of his own officers, reserving to himself as the one on whom the ultimate accountability would rest, the right of maintaining a supervision of it, or formally or informally interposing at need.[43]

And interpose he does, repeatedly and in such a manner as to make the trial seem little more than the rehearsal of a written script. So far as actual function is concerned, the members of the court are mere bystanders: Vere is at once Billy's accuser, his jury, and his judge. The officers he has chosen, not without some misgivings

[40] *Ibid.*, p. 704.
[41] *Ibid.*, p. 707.
[42] *Ibid.*, p. 703; see also p. 711.
[43] *Ibid.*, pp. 707-8.

of their good nature,[44] are simple, honest, and modest men, "without the faculty, [almost without] the inclination to gainsay one whom they [feel] to be an earnest man, one too not less their superior in mind than in naval rank."[45] As a result, Vere is able to manipulate them as he will, reducing the moral problem to a mere question of the mechanical infraction of a law, misrepresenting their desire for justice as overscrupulosity or baseless sentiment, confusing the issue by making the real question of the prisoner's intent seem to depend upon an understanding (by definition impossible) of "the mystery of iniquity" in Claggart, and — which proves decisive with them — impressing them with his own fears of "the practical consequences" of either an acquittal or a mitigation of the full penalty.[46] "In brief, Billy Budd was formally convicted and sentenced to be hung at the yard-arm in the early morning-watch...."[47]

It is sometimes argued in Vere's defense that his fears, viewed in context and without the benefit of hindsight, are entirely reasonable and proper: he has not simply imagined either the revolutionary unrest of Europe or the recent mutinies in the British fleet. And if this is so, his defenders continue, the action he takes must be considered both wise and courageous: he has no other meaningful alternative.

Now to argue in this way is of course to beg the question of the rightness of expediency as a principle of action. The conclusion follows from the given premise only for him whose watch is set to China time. Another man, less firmly committed to the ultimate value of particular institutions, might admit Vere's estimate of the situation to be entirely correct and yet regard his choice of a course of action as unquestionably wrong.

But coming down, as White-Jacket offered to do in the manner of flogging,[48] "from the lofty mast-head of an eternal principle" to the practical level of the quarter-deck, one may note in *Billy Budd* several passages that seem plainly intended to cast doubt on the necessity for Vere's action even on grounds of expediency.

For one, Vere has not the least grain of particular evidence that disaffection actually exists aboard his ship. Claggart, for all his "ferreting genius" and his obvious wish to frighten his commander,

---

[44] *Ibid.,* p. 708.
[45] *Ibid.,* pp. 717-18.
[46] *Ibid.,* pp. 711-12, 714-15, 712-14, 718, 716-17.
[47] *Ibid.,* p. 719.
[48] *White-Jacket,* p. 184 (chap. xxxvi).

has been able to bring forward nothing of a specific nature beyond his vague charge against Billy — which charge Vere does not believe.[49] Nor does the reader — and surely this is no oversight on Melville's part — have any evidence withheld from the captain. The general situation, it is true, is such as to justify watchfulness, but not alarm.[50] Mere possibility is a long step from near-certainty of impending revolt which moves Vere at the trial to insist upon the death penalty.[51] The *might-be*, like the *might-have been*, "is but boggy ground to build on."[52] Vere's surmise gains little support from the behavior of the men at those three later moments when the greatest strain is placed upon their loyalties. They receive his announcement of the death sentence with the unprotesting "dumbness . . . of a seated congregation of believers in hell listening to the clergyman's announcement of his Calvinistic text."[53] At the moment of Billy's execution, they echo, like good Calvinists, "with one voice from alow and aloft," the prisoner's last cry, " 'God bless Captain Vere!' "[54] And when their shipmate's body is tipped into the sea, their mood appears less one of anger against their officers than of awe before the seeming prodigies of Billy's peaceful death and that strange "croaked requiem" of the seabirds continuing to circle "the burial-spot astern."[55] Taking all in all, it is hard to see in the captain's fears anything more than the fantasies of a mind by nature somewhat pedantically abstract[56] and by the usages of office walled off from any direct contact with the particular realities of life aboard his ship.

But were one to admit the existence of latent discontent aboard the "Indomitable," one could still question the assertion that Vere has no reasonable alternative to the course he takes. He himself, before the convoking of the court, briefly considers one such alternative: to defer "taking any action whatever respecting it, further than to keep the foretopman a close prisoner till the ship [now on detached duty] rejoined the squadron and then submitting the matter to the judgment of his Admiral."[57] The same has already occurred, and independently, to the ship's officers and to the sur-

---

49 *Billy Budd,* in *The Portable Melville,* 695-98.
50 *Ibid.,* pp. 656-57.
51 *Ibid.,* p. 717.
52 *Ibid.,* p. 655.
53 *Ibid.,* p. 722.
54 *Ibid.,* p. 729.
55 *Ibid.,* p. 733.
56 *Ibid.,* p. 661.
57 *Ibid.,* p. 707.

geon, the latter at least a man most guarded in the drawing of inferences.[58] But Captain Vere dismisses the thought almost as soon as it comes, "feeling that unless quick action were [to be] taken on it, the deed of the Foretopman, so soon as it should be known on the gun-decks, would tend to awaken any slumbering embers of the Nore among the crew."[59] The word *any* seems not without significance here: Vere knows of no such embers; but he is fearful, and that fear itself dictates a secrecy which forbids his seeking evidence.[60] He is in this not unlike Claggart whose covert hatred, feeding upon a suspected injury, by its very "secretiveness voluntarily cuts [itself] off from enlightenment or disillusion; and, not unreluctantly, action is taken upon surmise as upon certainty."[61]

A still stronger indication of the narrator's belief that an alternative — and a practicable alternative — exists is given us, with an elaborate apology for "divergence" from "the main road," in the implied comparison of Vere and Lord Nelson.[62] Although Vere is nowhere explicitly compared with the admiral, the qualities attributed to this " 'greatest sailor since the world began' " bring the lesser man's own qualities, by the force of contrast, unavoidably to mind.[63] When we read of Nelson's almost vainglorious splendor of appearance, we are reminded of Vere's civilian look, his "unobtrusiveness of demeanor," as of "some highly honorable discreet envoy" visiting the quarter-deck.[64] The description of Nelson as a "reckless declarer of his person in fight" reminds us that Vere is "intrepid to the verge of temerity, but never injudiciously so."[65] Nelson — for all that he is "painfully circumspect" in his preparations for battle—invites by his rashness and bravado the reproof of the "martial utilitarians" and "the Benthamites of war."[66] The lodging of such a charge against Captain Vere would strike us as preposterous; but he does not by this immunity rise in our estimation: "Personal prudence, even when dictated by quite other than selfish considerations, surely is no special virtue in a military man;

---

[58] *Ibid.*, p. 704-5, 730-31.
[59] *Ibid.*, p. 707.
[60] *Ibid.*, pp. 698-99, 706-7.
[61] *Ibid.*, p. 680.
[62] *Ibid.*, pp. 653-57.
[63] The quoted phrase is twice repeated (*ibid.*, pp. 653, 655), as if for emphasis. We may note also that the guarded praise of Vere by his fellow officers (*ibid.*, p. 661) is so phrased as to invite the comparison with Lord Nelson.
[64] *Ibid.*, pp. 656, 658.
[65] *Ibid.*, pp. 655, 658.
[66] *Ibid.*, pp. 654-55.

while an excessive love of glory, impassioning a less burning impulse[,] the honest sense of duty, is the first."[67]

But all this is in preparation for the passage which most unmistakably points up the contrast between the two men:

> Discontent foreran the Two Mutinies, and more or less it lurk-
> ingly survived them. Hence it was not unreasonable to apprehend
> some return of trouble sporadic or general. One instance of such
> apprehensions: In the same year with this story, Nelson, then Vice-
> Admiral Sir Horatio, being with the fleet off the Spanish coast, was
> directed by the Admiral in command to shift his pennant from the
> *Captain* to the *Theseus*; and for this reason: that the latter ship
> having newly arrived on the station from home where it had taken
> part in the Great Mutiny, danger was apprehended from the temper
> of the men; and it was thought that an officer like Nelson was the
> one, not indeed to terrorise the crew into base subjection, but to win
> them, by force of his mere presence and heroic personality, back
> to an allegiance, if not as enthusiastic as his own, yet as true. So it
> was that for a time on more than one quarter-deck anxiety did
> exist.[68]

But how different the actions to which these apprehensions led!
To " 'respect the omens of ill' " is of course never unreasonable:
" 'evil is the chronic malady of the universe; and checked in one
place, breaks forth in another.' "[69] So "discontent" in some sense
"lurkingly survived" its suppression at the Nore, and the possibility
of its reappearance is something no responsible commander can
safely ignore. This much is true. But what is perhaps " 'the grand
error' " of Captain Vere, as of other doctrinaire and wholly committed men, is " 'the general supposition, that the very special
Diabolus is abroad; whereas, the very special Diabolus has been
abroad ever since [the world] began.' "[70] The year A.D. 1797 is not
the first time the world has stood in crisis:

---

[67] *Ibid.,* p. 655.

[68] *Ibid.,* pp. 656-57. One may recall also that in an earlier book of Melville's,
"the Great Sailor" is called to the stand as an expert witness against flogging,
a mode of discipline to which Vere (*ibid.,* pp. 666-67) has shown himself not
wholly averse: "It is well known that Lord Nelson himself, in point of policy,
was averse to flogging; and that, too, when he had witnessed the mutinous
effects of government abuses in the navy . . . which to the terror of all England, developed themselves at the great mutiny of the Nore: an outbreak that
for several weeks jeopardized the very existence of the British navy" (*White-
Jacket,* p. 186, chap. xxxvi).

[69] *Mardi,* II, 244 (chap. clxi).

[70] *Ibid.,* p. 238 (chap. clxi).

> "By Fate's decree
> Have not earth's vitals heaved in change
> Repeated? some wild element
> Or action been evolved? the range
> Of surface split? the deeps unpent?
> Continents in God's cauldrons cast?
> And this without effecting so
> The neutralising of the past,
> Whose rudiments persistent flow,
> From age to age transmitting, own,
> The evil with the good."[71]

And if the world has rallied from these convulsions sufficiently to continue, this is to be credited less to human foresight than to the presence, in that "persistent flow," of a " 'good which lets [the] evil last.' "[72] Since no man reads the future, "let us revere that sacred uncertainty which forever impends over men and nations."[73] The ebb and flow of good and evil is a movement to be traced not only in the general advance and retreat of tides but in the thrust and withdrawal of each separate wave. Melville found this truth of sufficient importance to what he was saying in *Billy Budd* for him to devote his entire preface to it:[74]

---

[71] *Clarel,* I, 137 (Part I, canto xxxiv).

[72] *Ibid.,* II, 240 (Part IV, canto xix).

[73] "Supplement" to *Battle-Pieces,* in Poems, p. 186.

[74] Since these pages first appeared in print, Harrison Hayford and Merton M. Sealts, Jr. have shown, in a careful analysis of Melville's manuscript in their *Billy Budd, Sailor (An Inside Narrative)* (University of Chicago Press, 1962; pp. 9-10, 18-19, 25, 259-260, 377-382) that previous editors have been mistaken in accepting as the author's "Preface" the passage quoted here. As their "Genetic Text" makes clear, it was originally written to follow a version of Chapter 19 that ended with the Surgeon reflecting upon the self defeating prudence of Vere's secrecy in the matter of Claggart's death; but in a later radical revision of the chapter it was removed by the author, put into a separate folder at the end of the manuscript, and left with no direction as to re-location. Their evidence in support of this point seems to me conclusive, and their decision to remove the passage from the front of the work is entirely justified. I cannot, however, join in their apparent feeling that the substance and relevance of the passage, as well as its traditional placement, have been invalidated by their discovery. The misnamed "Preface" still seems to me a significant and relevant object of study for anyone attempting to understand *Billy Budd,* and it ought therefore, I feel, to remain readily available to students together with a statement of its relation to the manuscript. In the generally admirable Hayford-Sealts edition it is not thus available. The editors appear to regard it as a mere "discarded fragment" (p. 25) that contributes little or nothing to our understanding of what Melville is about. They have accordingly excluded it not merely from their "Reading Text" (which is right) but from the "Notes and Commentary" where it properly belongs, thus

The opening proposition made by the Spirit of that Age, involved the rectification of the Old World's hereditary wrongs. In France to some extent this was bloodily effected. But what then? Straightway the Revolution itself became a wrongdoer, one more oppressive than the Kings. Under Napoleon it enthroned upstart kings, and initiated that prolonged agony of continual war whose final throe was Waterloo. During those years not the wisest could have foreseen that the outcome of all would be what to some thinkers apparently it has since turned out to be, a political advance along nearly the whole line for Europeans.

Now as elsewhere hinted, it was something caught from the Revolutionary Spirit that at Spithead emboldened the man-of-war's men to rise against real abuses, long-standing ones, and afterwards at the Nore to make inordinate and aggressive demands, successful resistance to which was confirmed only when the ringleaders were

---

putting it wholly out of the reach of the general reader (who presumably has only the paperback issue of their edition) and forcing the scholar to reconstruct it for himself, word by painful word, from the necessarily cryptic "Genetic Text" in the library edition. Yet this seemingly worthless passage is (by the editors' own evidence) not merely of Melville's authorship but was composed late in the writing of *Billy Budd* and, though removed by him from its first location in or just after Chapter 19, neither destroyed nor cancelled nor recast in different form but (like the canonically received Chapters 4 and 7) set aside in a folder—for what discernible purpose but eventual relocation? As it was not "discarded" by Melville but merely set aside, so (I would argue) it is no "fragment" but an organized and coherent whole whose meaning is perfectly consonant with much else in the story, specifically with the substance of Chapter 3. It has as its subject the indeterminate and ambiguous character of events in both the immediate and the larger contexts of history, and not, as Hayford and Sealts suggest in their introduction (pp. 9-10) the difficulty that "existing circumstances in the navy" pose for Captain Vere. Commenting there on a single sentence quoted from the "Preface," the editors observe: "It was on the basis of these reflections that the narrator then in effect underwrote Vere's view of the case, doing so in the course of an extended passage still standing in the final manuscript (Leaves 228-45). . . ." Readers of *Billy Budd* are free to judge for themselves whether the pages indicated actually do constitute an endorsement by the narrator of Vere's position. But in the absence of a full and clear text of the "Preface," it is not in their power to judge whether it was reached "on the basis of these reflections."

Clearly the disputed passage is not an integral part of the novel as it stands, and no responsible critic will base his interpretation simply upon it as an initial statement "intended to establish a basic tone and point of reference for the entire novel." But is it not permissible to conclude that in writing it Melville was making an important comment upon the complexity of events at the moment of Vere's short-sighted choice? And may we not suppose that his later removal of the passage was prompted by aesthetic rather than philosophical second thoughts? In studying a work of the moral complexity and evident unfinished state of *Billy Budd,* it would seem appropriate to look for traces of the builder's intent even among the unplaced or half-shaped stones left at the site. But if we are to do this, they must remain accessible for us.

hung for an admonitory spectacle to the anchored fleet. Yet in a way analogous to the operation of the Revolution at large the Great Mutiny, though by Englishmen naturally deemed monstrous at the time, doubtless gave the first latent prompting to most important reforms in the British Navy.[75]

Could one forbid events, as the censor forbids books, the task of choosing those events would not be easy. For "in all things man sows upon the wind, which bloweth just where it listeth; for ill or good, man cannot know. Often ill comes from the good, as good from the ill."[76]

There is a sense in which *Benito Cereno* and *Billy Budd* may be said to complement each other. Each is essentially a study in blindness: as Captain Delano in the one is blind to the strength and permanence of evil, so in the other Captain Vere cannot see that good has the power to maintain itself, if never wholly to prevail, in a world where it seems always at the point of extinction. Still less does Vere realize that it is by its own intrinsic power that it survives and not through any devices borrowed from its opposite. The good which in this instance eventually comes from the evil of the young sailor's death owes nothing at all to Vere's supposed foresight — with regard to which that death must appear wholly futile and meaningless — and everything to the simple fact of Billy's own goodness silently operating upon the hearts of men. It is the crowning weakness of expediency that it so often turns out not to have been expedient at all. Captain Vere, dying of his wound at Gibraltar, is perhaps fortunate in being cut off before attaining to this humiliating knowledge and to the remorse which must have followed it.[77] The rest of us, realizing what little control man has over the consequences of his actions, may find in Vere's story encouragement to risk the luxury of at least following our own conscience.

---

[75] *Billy Budd,* in *The Portable Melville,* pp. 637-38.
[76] "The Encantadas," in *The Piazza Tales,* p. 227.
[77] *Billy Budd,* in *The Portable Melville,* p. 736.

Anne McNamara

"Melville's *Billy Budd*"

Student complaints about the frequency of classical reference in *Billy Budd* are reduced by demonstration of the purely functional quality of Melville's use of Greek myth. References to the Graces, Love, Apollo, Hyperion, Hercules, the Vestals, and the Fates cumulatively present and emphasize the sublimity and grandeur of the young foretopman's character.

To say that Billy's looks and movements suggested a mother "eminently favored by Love and the Graces" (Chap. II) is to impute to him an inheritance of personal radiance, happiness, warmth, and love of fellowman; for Aglaia, Euphrosyne, and Thalia (Graces), personifying Brilliance, Joy, and Bloom, inspired in men the natural charm of love, understanding, sociability, and pleasant address. To refer to Billy as Apollo (I) and Hyperion (XV), epithets often misconstrued as mere hackneyed titles for his manly beauty and gracious superiority, is to elevate this endowment, charging it with godlike benignity and gracious magnanimity, for Apollo was identified with Helios, the sun-god, and Hyperion, a

From *The Explicator*, xxi, No. 2 (October 1962). Reprinted by permission. Copyright 1962 by *The Explicator*.

Titan son of Uranus, was father of that bright deity. To associate Billy with fabulous Hercules, "strong man" of Greece (II), not only intensifies Billy's abnormal physical strength but also calls attention to the superior moral sense that commanded it, emphasizing his controlled potency and confident self-containment. Moreover, this sweetness-strength pattern (Apollo-Hyperion-Graces-Hercules) is heightened by Apollo's role as god of music and poetry, lover of Calliope ("the beautiful-voiced"), and father of Orpheus, famous Thracian poet and musician, whose melodies charmed birds and animals and gave sweet speech to stones. Thus raised above the "natural regality" of the traditional Handsome Sailor (I), Billy-Apollo is not only a hero in stature and a god in aspect and disposition but also a kind of primitive bard, who can sing and compose "like the illiterate nightingale" (II). His pacific effect on the crew of the *Rights* (I) and his generous cry at the moment of execution on the *Indomitable* may well be foreshadowed in the Apollo-nightingale references, for the bird image recurs in the hanging scene to figure the "phenomenal effect" of the "rare" and "spiritualized" beauty of the boy, the harmony audible in the shocked crew's echoing his "God bless Captain Vere!" (XXIV)

Again, in the accusation scene (XIX), the smile of the Vestal priestess is brilliantly functional in suggesting Billy's innocence, devotion, and suffering. Like a Vestal, he is virgin, constant in tending the hearth-flame (brotherly love and peace) among his people (crew) and in his city (ship), and subject to death under law. Like her, he struggles inarticulately against "suffocation," as the weight of Claggart's vicious lie begins to "bury him alive" in Vere's official justice (XIX).

Finally, references to the Fates and implications of the operation of *hamartia* (tragic flaw) foreshadow the inescapable death sentence of Billy the "fatalist" (I). Into Vere's "Fated boy!" (XIX) crowd all the ancient, foreboding stories of Clotho the Spinner, Lachesis the Measurer, and Atropos the Inflexible Cutter, inexorable dispensers of man's destiny. Billy is "nipped in the vise of fate" (XXIV), caught between evil incarnate (Claggart) and the single "imperfection" in his own beautiful nature (II): "I had to say something, and I could only say it with a blow." (XXI)

Major functional elements in Melville's presentation of Billy Budd's physical and moral character, exquisitely appropriate to his concept of his hero as a "pre-Christian saint," these classical references are neither pedantic, decorative, nor expendable.

Harrison Hayford and Merton M. Sealts, Jr.

From *Billy Budd, Sailor (An Inside Narrative)*

Growth of the Manuscript

The manuscript of *Billy Budd* as Melville left it at his death in 1891 may be most accurately described as a semi-final draft, not a final fair copy ready for publication. After his death Mrs. Melville, indeed, called the story "unfinished." She had used exactly the same word in December of 1885 when reporting Melville's retirement from his nineteen years of employment as a customs inspector: "He has a great deal [of] unfinished work at his desk which will give him occupation." The "unfinished work" of 1885 may have included the short poem of three or four leaves on which he was working early in 1886, the poem that ultimately became the ballad "Billy in the Darbies" with which the novel concludes. The novel itself developed out of a brief prose headnote setting the scene and introducing the speaker of this poem. An understanding of

From the Editors' Introduction to *Billy Budd, Sailor (An Inside Narrative)*, ed. Harrison Hayford and Merton M. Sealts, Jr. (Chicago: University of Chicago Press, 1962), pp. 1-3, 33-39. Reprinted by permission of The University of Chicago Press. © 1962 by The University of Chicago. All rights reserved.

just how the story took form during the last five years of its author's life has been a major objective of our genetic study of the *Billy Budd* manuscript.

As *Billy Budd* grew under Melville's hand, along with other works both in prose and in verse with which he was engaged, it passed through several distinct stages and substages of development that comprised three major phases, in each of which its original focus was radically altered. Our genetic analysis has followed the course of its growth from the surviving leaves of the ballad and its headnote to Melville's late pencil revisions of his semi-final draft. It has established the fact that more than once, believing his work to be essentially complete, he undertook to put his manuscript into fair-copy form, but each time he was led into further revision and elaboration; what still further changes he might have made had he lived to continue work on the manuscript are of course conjectural. The following section outlines the main phases of the story's development, as established by our analysis of the manuscript. The degree to which *Billy Budd* remained an "unfinished" work is a matter for critical evaluation in the light of detailed evidence assembled in the table and discussion accompanying our Genetic Text.

Early in 1886, when Melville took up, or perhaps began, the work that became *Billy Budd*, he had in mind neither the plot of a novel nor any one of the characters as they later emerged in the course of his writing. What he did have, in the initial phase of development now represented by four extant draft leaves (Plates I-IV), was a short composition in both prose and verse that in its complete form ran to perhaps five or six leaves. The focal character was Billy (Billy Budd in the prose headnote), a sailor on the eve of his execution — but a different Billy from the young sailor of the novel who is hanged for striking and killing his superior officer. This Billy was an older man, condemned for fomenting mutiny and apparently guilty as charged, though in his brief initial presentation Melville emphasized the sailor's reverie as he faces death, rather than the events leading up to his condemnation. The prose sketch and ballad thus placed a character in a situation but stopped short of telling a story.

During the first two years of Melville's retirement, 1886-87, a narrative about Billy Budd emerged out of this material. By November of 1888 Melville had incorporated the ballad and expanded the headnote sketch through several stages into a story that ran to something over 150 manuscript leaves. In constructing its plot he had entered a second phase of development with his introduction of John Claggart, whose presence resulted in a major shift of focus. Billy, no mutineer in this phase, reacts to a false charge of mutiny by striking and killing his accuser, Claggart; this is the act that leads to his condemnation here and in all subsequent stages of the story's growth.

A third and final phase of development, during which the manuscript grew to its ultimate length of 351 leaves, began after November, 1888, when Melville set out (not for the first time) to put his story into fair-copy form. During the ensuing winter months or perhaps in the following spring he made another major shift of focus, which involved the full-scale delineation of a third principal character, Captain the Honorable Edward Fairfax Vere, who had previously figured only as the commander in whose presence Billy struck Claggart and by whom the summary sentence of hanging was imposed upon the young sailor. So minor was this commander's part in the second phase of the story's growth that only a few leaves stood between the killing of Claggart and the beginning of the ballad; in the third phase, by contrast, Billy's trial, Vere's long speech to the court, and the dramatized execution and related episodes intervene, and an analysis of Vere's character is now provided in new antecedent chapters. The several stages and substages within this final phase of development occupied Melville until the end of his life, revision being still in progress when he died.

Thus, in the period of over five years between his retirement from the Custom House and his death, Melville had carried the work through a series of developments intricate in detail but clear in their general lines of growth. In three main phases he had introduced in turn the three main characters: first Billy, then Claggart, and finally Vere. As the focus of his attention shifted from one to another of these three principals, the plot and thematic emphasis of the expanding novel underwent consequent modifications within each main phase. Just where the emphasis finally lay in the not altogether finished story as he left it is, in essence, the issue that has engaged and divided the critics of *Billy Budd.*

.   .   .

Perspectives for Criticism

Our Genetic Text opens various possibilities for . . . internal study of *Billy Budd* both in the process of creation and in its end state. Beyond the broad phases of development outlined in the first section of this Introduction, what was the retired customs inspector, who had long ago written *Moby Dick*, accomplishing in the leisurely process of proliferating revision that occupied his "quiet, grass-growing" last years, a process terminated by the death of the author rather than the completion of his manuscript? In many of the late pieces, it would appear, he accomplished little — he was puttering. In *Billy Budd*, however, he achieved a work that has entered the canon of major American fiction and is usually listed second to *Moby Dick* among his novels. Wherein lay the difference between *Billy Budd* and the other late pieces? Did its quality of greatness emerge with one transforming major stroke somewhere in the gradual process of growth by accretion? Were all the instances of his minute verbal revision necessary to its greatness, or were many of them merely nervous or fussy gestures? To what extent do the revisions show a sure intuition of what was vital in the work as it stood at the end in semi-final manuscript? To what extent are many of the revisions purely random strokes that overlie and obscure the emerging conception? Into what categories do the stylistic revisions fall? Similar questions about the process of revision will occur to every reader. Many problems relevant to interpretation and evaluation will likewise suggest themselves — interrelated problems about form, theme, and language, to which study of the Genetic Text may suggest answers.

In conclusion, by way of example, we wish to open one suggestive line of analysis in order to show the bearing of our genetic study upon the problem of tone and focus occasioned by the crucial late revisions.

It seems fair to say that were it not for the effect of Melville's late pencil revisions (as summarized above, pp. 9-11) the critical controversy of the last dozen years over the story's tone in relation to Vere and his actions would scarcely have arisen. Even those interpreters who disapprove Vere's course could not well question the author's evident design as revealed at Stage *Ga*, to establish that course in terms of "existing conditions in the navy." The cumulative effect — whatever the intention — of his subsequent deletions and insertions, however, was to throw into doubt not only the rightness of Vere's decision and the soundness of his mind but also the narrator's own position concerning him. As the revised sequence now stands, it is no longer as narrator but in terms of the surgeon's reflections that Melville introduces the reaction to Vere and his plan to place Billy on trial. He leaves the narrator pointedly noncommittal, telling the reader in so many words that he must decide for himself concerning the captain's state of mind. Yet in the unmodified paragraphs that Melville allowed to stand immediately after the surgeon's reflections, the narrator presents Vere's position in a sympathetic tone (Leaves 238-45). Also, following the narrator's allusion to the *Somers* case as "History, and here cited without comment," Melville retained a quotation from "a writer whom few know" (obviously Melville himself), the tenor of which is exculpatory, or at worst extenuative. The next chapter (Ch. 22), also retained after the revision, reports Vere's closeted interview with Billy in a tone unmistakably favorable to the captain. In sum, it is the late revisions — those involving the surgeon — which raise doubts; those passages composed earlier which are still retained tend to represent Vere favorably.

What, then, did Melville suppose was the effect of his late revisions? What attitude was he himself taking when he made them? Had he in fact completed them? And what may a reader make of them?

If only in view of the narrator's reservations (at both stages) concerning Vere's "maintenance of secrecy" in the case (Leaf 242), it would seem unwise to infer, as some readers have done, that Melville's final attitude toward Vere was one of unequivocal endorsement. Conversely, if the "prudent surgeon" was intended to replace the narrator as a spokesman for the author himself, the reader would of course conclude that Melville too condemned Vere's position. But it is not justifiable to take the revisions simply in that light.

For one thing, there are the retained passages, pointed out above, in which the narrator's tone and comments are sympathetic to Vere. For another thing, given the near-caricature of the surgeon embodied in Ch. 26 (inscribed earlier at Stage *F/G*), which emphasizes his unimaginative obtuseness — in line with Melville's usual treatment of doctors and other "men of science" — it is hardly justifiable to take his views of Vere as embodying Melville's own. And for a third thing, one obvious point of the revisions was to re-emphasize the important theme, already otherwise developed in various ways, that to such ordinary minds as the surgeon's, or those of the officers of the court, such truly "exceptional natures" as any of the three principals — Billy and Claggart as well as Vere — are in effect closed books. Thus the surgeon's attitude toward Vere's behavior parallels his obtuse attitude toward the "phenomenal" lack of motion in Billy's suspended body.

A final and major point is that in making the revision Melville was doing what he had consistently done in the whole course of composition: he was *dramatizing* the situation (and its implications) which he had previously *reported*. The point may be served by a quotation from Charles Olson (1948), who preferred Freeman's composite "Baby Budd" to the supposedly later *Billy Budd*, as more dramatic. In expanding the story, Olson declared, Melville "worked over and over as though the hand that wrote was Hawthorne's, with his essayism, his hints, the veil of his syntax, until the celerity of the short story was run out, the force of the juxtapositions interrupted, and the secret of Melville as artist, the presentation of ambiguity by the event direct, was lost in the Salem manner." Actually, as we have shown, *Billy Budd* developed in almost the opposite way, from exposition into dramatization. Yet the terms of Olson's criticism, if not the conclusions, are highly relevant.

Both of the conspicuous developments in the third and final phase — the prominent role now given to Vere and the revised role given to the surgeon — arose when Melville transformed what had been statements and implications into dramatic terms. The first development, that of Vere's new role, was entailed in Melville's creation of the trial scene. This scene dramatized the same considerations that had dictated Billy's execution from the Stage A headnote onward — not only his naval crime but the officers' apprehensions of the spread of mutiny. (Thus, in a sense, Vere's position was predetermined by the nature of the situation addressed from the start, though the quality of Vere's awareness of that position was not.) The scene also dramatized the conflict of military duty with human feeling, which from the beginning was a generating source of the story's pathos. This conflict had already been shaped through the series of more or less congruent dichotomies that inform the story (nature versus society, feeling versus reason, rights-of-man versus ordered forms, Christian morality versus war, and so on). By means of the trial scene the hitherto diffused conflict was brought into dramatic focus, in the breasts of the court of officers, and most of all in Captain Vere's intense realization of the claims of both sides. The peculiar fervor of his argument to the reluctant officers is generated by the conflict working within himself.

The preservation of two superseded leaves enables us to observe in some detail the way in which Melville dramatized one passage in the trial scene. The leaves (from Stage C) are those of the superseded digressive chapter "Lawyers, Experts, Clergy" (Leaves [135a]353, [135b]354). There Melville had speculated, "by the way," upon the problem offered courts by such evil natures as he

Billy Budd, Sailor

had attributed to Claggart and associated with the biblical "mystery of iniquity" (Leaf 135). "Can it be the phenomenon," he asked, "that in some criminal cases puzzles the courts? For this cause have our juries at times not only to endure the prolonged contentions of lawyers with their fees but also the yet more perplexing strife of the medical experts with theirs?" And he went on, "But why leave it to them? why not subpoena as well the clerical proficients?" Later, dramatizing this speculation at Stage X, Melville created a court scene that gave an immediacy to precisely these questions. The thoughtful marine officer, in effect a juror in a criminal case, is presented as puzzled just so by Claggart's motivation: "Why should he have so lied, so maliciously lied," he asks Billy, "since you declare there was no malice between you?" The question touches on "a spiritual sphere wholly obscure to Billy's thoughts," as indeed to those of the marine captain and his colleagues. But Vere, who is presented as a character capable of divining that sphere, answers in terms taken over directly from Melville's own earlier speculations quoted above: "Ay, there is a mystery," he says, "but, to use a scriptural phrase, it is a 'mystery of iniquity,' a matter for psychologic theologians to discuss" (Leaves 258-59). Vere's next speech is also drawn from the earlier pasage on "clerical proficients" who "know something about those intricacies involved in the question of moral responsibility"; in this next speech he admits Billy's case is an exceptional one which "well might be referred to a jury of casuists." A civil court, it was said in the earlier phrase already quoted, must "endure the prolonged contentions" of such experts; now Vere, to whose speech Melville adapted the phrase, objects that "strangely we prolong proceedings" (Leaf 257) and insists that the military court must act summarily. One further motif of the "Lawyers, Experts, Clergy" chapter remained to be salvaged — Melville's slurs on "the medical experts" who for fees directly contradict each other. This motif, in effect, he partly dramatized in the obtuse surgeon who, not understanding the cause of his captain's unwonted behavior, "professionally and privately surmised" that he was the sudden victim of mental aberration. Partly, also, Melville repeated the slur in the same passage with the surgeon's surmise: "to draw the exact line of demarcation few will undertake, though for a fee . . . some professional experts will."

Thus the late pencil revision involving the surgeon followed a process Melville had repeatedly engaged in from the beginning. The process was very likely that by which (during Stage A) he had converted his original headnote summary and character sketch of

Billy Budd into a plotted story, though of that transformation we have no direct evidence. Certainly it was the process by which he had turned into scenes his narrative statements of such events as Billy's impressment, his ignorance of his paternity, and Claggart's use of understrappers to harass Billy.

All along, Melville's dramatization had the effect, among others, of dissociating the narrator from commitments he had earlier made or positions that Melville might wish to insinuate without endorsing. Although this effect of noncommittal "alienation" was sometimes incidental to his dramatizations, it was often — perhaps usually — deliberately sought. A transparent example is the attribution of the commentary on Vere's course at the end of Ch. 21 to "a writer whom few know" (earlier to "a writer whom nobody knows, and who being dead recks not of the oblivion") — the writer obviously being Melville himself. The "honest scholar, my senior" (Leaves 127-30) falls in the same class. Similarly, but more effectively, Melville created the Dansker as a shrewd and experienced old man to whom to assign speculations concerning "what might eventually befall a nature" such as Billy's when "dropped into a world" as oddly incongruous with it as the warship's environment (Leaves 110-11). A telling example may be cited in the scene between the captain and the surgeon: in the earlier version the narrator himself equates Billy's fatal blow with "the divine judgment on Ananias"; in the revised version Melville gives the phrase to Captain Vere as a sudden dramatic exclamation — one of those which arouse the surgeon's disquietude. The effect, analogously, of many of Melville's stylistic revisions is to achieve the same "pithy, guarded" tone as the Dansker's comments, if not their "cynicism." "The secret of Melville as artist" Charles Olson defined as "the presentation of ambiguity by the event direct." The whole episode involving the surgeon is a complex example of Melville's working toward direct presentation, and the effect was certainly, in the end, one of ambiguity. Other means than direct presentation, however, contribute to that effect, among them the guarded, noncommittal statements by the narrator.

Also contributing to the effect of ambiguity, it may be suggested, are what must be described genetically as inconsistencies.* That these inconsistencies merge, in their effect, with the ambiguities is

---

*In making his late revisions Melville had also introduced certain inconsistencies and uncertainties (if not outright contradictions) as to what, according to "usage," was the captain's proper course under the circumstances. See note to Leaf 233, *a drumhead court*, which also adduces statutes of the period applicable to such a case.

not altogether fortuitous. In raising, through the surgeon's reactions and his "private and professional" surmises, some question about Vere's course and even his sanity, Melville was deliberately dissociating the narrator from commitment and throwing "cross-lights" upon Vere. The disagreements and prolonged contentions among what Melville might have called "the critical experts" are but the proper issue of his requiring every reader to "determine for himself." But the rhetorical question "Who in the rainbow can draw the line . . . ?" should be a warning to critics who find the lines of demarcation in the story easy to determine and who suppose Melville's own attitude was altogether clear cut. To Melville's mind, after all, the question was not simply the rightness or wrongness, sanity or insanity, of the captain's action, but also the very existence of a problematical world in which such a story as he had been so long developing and brooding upon was (in his guarded phrase) "not unwarranted." His story was an epitome, in art, of such a world.

Would Melville himself, in a "finished" version of *Billy Budd*, perhaps have removed the inconsistencies, if not have resolved the ambiguities, concerning the captain? And more fundamentally, would he have undertaken further adjustments of emphasis among his three principals? Only conjectural answers are possible, of course. In our judgment, however, these questions, posed by our analysis of the manuscript and study of its development, bring critical debate about the work into a new perspective: Was the story as it stood when Melville died (and as we have now presented it in our edited Reading Text) complete in all significant respects though "unfinished" in details? Or, on the other hand, was it, because still under revision at a passage crucially affecting its tone and focus (and perhaps for other reasons as well), radically "unfinished"? In short, is *Billy Budd* a unified work of art?

A possible—and appropriately ambiguous—answer is suggested by Melville's own words in *Moby Dick:*

> . . . I now leave my cetological System standing thus unfinished, even as the great Cathedral of Cologne was left, with the crane still standing upon the top of the uncompleted tower. . . . God keep me from ever completing anything. This whole book is but a draught— nay, but the draught of a draught. Oh, Time, Strength, Cash, and Patience! (Ch. 32)

Perhaps the "unfinished" *Billy Budd* should be regarded in this light. Melville's often declared conception of the relation between reality and literature, between "truth" and the writer's attempt to see and state it, involved both incompletion and formal imperfection as a necessity: a work that is faithful to reality *must* in the end be both incomplete and unshapely, since truth is both elusive and intractable and the writer is limited in "Time, Strength, Cash, and Patience." "Truth uncompromisingly told," he wrote near the end of *Billy Budd*, "will always have its ragged edges; hence the conclusion of such a narration is apt to be less finished than an architectural finial."

H. Bruce Franklin

From *The Wake of the Gods*

He has also the name of Budd, Victory, and Buddugre, *the* "god of victory, the king who rises in light, and ascends the sky."
SIR EDWARD DAVIES, *The Mythology and Rites of the British Druids*

They call their God Budd, the God of Victory, the king who rises in light and ascends the sky.
GODFREY HIGGINS, *Anacalypsis*

. . . Bili Buada *or* Bile *of Victory, whose name possibly meant victorious Death.*
JOHN RHYS, *Lectures on the Origin and Growth of Religion as Illustrated by Celtic Heathendom*

Billy Budd is Melville's last word on the myths of man. In it he describes the making of an idol, a god, and a myth — Billy Budd, who is a man and a god created by man.

Billy Budd opens and closes with the image of a being worshiped by sailors. In the beginning, the black African Handsome Sailor,

Reprinted from *The Wake of the Gods: Melville's Mythology,* by H. Bruce Franklin (Stanford: Stanford University Press, 1963), pp. 188-189, 191-202, with the permission of the publishers, Stanford University Press. © 1963 by the Board of Trustees of the Leland Stanford Junior University.

worshiped like the grand sculptured bull of the Assyrians, fades out and Billy Budd, the blond English Handsome Sailor, appears. In the end, other sailors create of Billy Budd a deity which transcends the Handsome Sailor idol of a single ship; Budd becomes their Christ. Explicit narrative statements label the sailors who adulate the African and English Handsome Sailors and the sailors who finally deify Budd as the ignorant, superstitious sailors who abounded in the time before steamships, that is, they belong to that group of primitives who created the myth of the White Whale. But the myth which the sailors in *Billy Budd* make does not destroy, but saves, them.

. . .

Billy Budd is the only one of Melville's protagonists who actually bears the name of a god. Curiously, he bears at one time the name of two gods. As Walter Sutton has pointed out in "Melville and the Great God Budd," elements of Buddhistic thought serve important functions in *Billy Budd.** But the Eastern god Budd is not Billy Budd's primary namesake: both his first name and his last name are names of a particular Western god upon whose mythology and rites Melville constructed *Billy Budd.* This god is the god known as "the Celtic Apollo."

Astronomical conflicts between the true sun-god and mock sun-gods result in much of the imagery in *Mardi;* the opposition between Ahab, the would-be sun-god, and the nature of the true sun and true sun-god creates some of the cosmic tensions in *Moby-Dick;* the Cosmopolitan equivocally suggests that he may or may not be the true sun and the true Apollo. As might be expected, the myth of the sun-god partly shapes Billy Budd's divinity. The sun-god myth was, of course, the myth upon which the heretical mythologists said that the story of Christ was founded, the myth which the apologists attempted to contrast with the Christ story. Greek mythology preserves this myth most coherently in Apollo, and, to a lesser degree, in Hyperion and Hercules. Billy Budd is compared explicitly to three gods, all Greek — Hyperion, Hercules, and Apollo. Of these three, Apollo is by far the most important. Hyperion yielded his dominion to Apollo; Hercules seems more man than god. Many mythologists therefore resolved all three into

---

*Many nineteenth-century comparative mythologists used "Budd" as a spelling of the name of the Buddhist god. According to Howard Vincent's reading of the text of "Rammon," Melville twice spells the name "Budda" (*Collected Poems,* pp. 412, 413).

one god, represented by Apollo, "the perfection of united manly strength and beauty."[1] Budd, the "angel of God" who strikes down Claggart, appropriately resembles Apollo, to whose darts were ascribed all sudden deaths of men, particularly the sudden deaths of evil men.[2] And Apollo, like Budd, slays the serpent.

The mythologists found that killing the serpent was a central act in the sun-god myth. The apologists struggled with the prophecy about Krishna, Christ's antecedent, and often called "the Indian Apollo," that he would bruise the serpent's head. The skeptics played games like the one Rolfe plays in *Clarel,* I, xxxi, when he telescopes Osiris, Christ, and Apollo into a single myth, even substituting Python, Apollo's reptilian foe, for Typhon-Set, the dismemberer of Osiris. As Maurice puts it, everywhere throughout Asia "was to be seen a god contending with his adversary, an envenomed serpent; Osiris, Hercules, Creeshna, and Apollo, are beheld alternately to aim at the slimy monster the victorious javelin, or wield a destroying club."[3]

The central act of *Billy Budd* comes when Budd slays the serpent. Earlier hints have implied that Claggart is the serpent of Eden. When he accuses Budd, Claggart becomes the reptilian incarnation of evil, the gliding demon hunted by Ahab:

> Meanwhile the accuser's eyes, removing not as yet from the blue dilated ones, underwent a phenomenal change, their wonted rich violet color blurring into a muddy purple. Those lights of human intelligence, losing human expression, were gelidly protruding like the alien eyes of certain uncatalogued creatures of the deep. The first mesmeristic glance was one of serpent fascination; the last was as the paralyzing lurch of the torpedo fish.[4]

Unlike Ahab, Budd can and does slay the demon. Claggart's dead body reveals his living nature: "The spare form flexibly acquiesced, but inertly. It was like handling a dead snake." Ahab is slain by the monster which he assails; in futilely trying to purge the seas of life of its gliding great demon, he destroys himself and his crew. Budd succeeds in slaying the monster, and he is therefore destroyed by man. But Budd attains not only victory over the ser-

---

[1] Charles Anthon, *A Classical Dictionary* (New York, 1854), "Apollo."
[2] See, for instance, Anthon's account.
[3] Thomas Maurice, *The History of Hindostan,* 2d ed., 3 vols. (London, 1819), II, 228.
[4] *Billy Budd: Sailor (An Inside Narrative)*, ed. Harrison Hayford and Merton M. Sealts, Jr. (Chicago, 1962), p. 98.

pent but also victory through his sacrifice over his destruction. And that is why he is named Budd, the *"god of victory,"* the Celtic Apollo."[5]

Billy Budd is a story about Britain and its navy, and about the values they symbolize. Billy Budd himself is a living embodiment of an elemental kind of Britishness. We most clearly see the essence of Budd's ancient and primitive Britishness in the passage which explains why "the good chaplain" cannot impress "the young barbarian" with Christian notions of death and why he cannot "bring home to him the thought of salvation and a Savior":

> Not that like children Billy was incapable of conceiving what death really is. No, but he was wholly without irrational fear of it, a fear more prevalent in highly civilized communities than those so-called barbarous ones which in all respects stand nearer to unadulterate Nature. And, as elsewhere said, a barbarian Billy radically was — as much so, for all the costume, as his countrymen the British captives, living trophies, made to march in the Roman triumph of Germanicus. Quite as much so as those later barbarians, young men probably, and picked specimens among the earlier British converts to Christianity, at least nominally such, taken to Rome (as today converts from lesser isles of the sea may be taken to London), of whom the Pope of that time, admiring the strangeness of their personal beauty so unlike the Italian stamp, their clear ruddy complexion and curled flaxen locks, exclaimed, "Angles" (meaning *English,* the modern derivative) "Angles, do you call them? And is it because they look so like angels?" (P. 120)

In describing these primitive and almost symbolic qualities of the ancient Britons, embodied by Billy Budd, Melville draws upon Polynesia, where he had seen "barbarism" and Christianity in conflict. The chaplain is received by Budd as "the primer of Christianity, full of transcendent miracles, was received long ago on tropic isles by any superior *savage,* so called — a Tahitian, say, of Captain Cook's time or shortly after that time." Billy Budd combines the ultimately primitive sailor, who is like the primitive Polynesian, with the ultimately primitive Briton, both Celtic and Teutonic, who is also like the primitive Polynesian. It should come as no surprise that in this context Melville, who thought of the Druids when he saw the stone ruins of the Typee valley, should

[5] Edward Davies, *The Mythology and Rites of the British Druids* (London, 1809), pp. 116, 120, 468, 584, 627; Godfrey Higgins, *Anacalypsis,* 2 vols. (London, 1836), I, 154.

think again of the Druids. And it was to Druidism that he went in quest of mythological and religious symbols appropriate to *Billy Budd*. The mythology and rites of the British Druids in large part define both the action and the symbolism of *Billy Budd*.

It is virtually impossible to pinpoint Melville's sources of information on the Druids. The Druids were discussed in detail by such ancient writers as Caesar, Pliny, Horace, Ammianus Marcellinus, Diodorus, Strabo, Lucan, Diogenes Laërtius, and Lucretius; English and Irish antiquarians had been publishing notes, articles, and books on the Druids for over two hundred years before *Billy Budd* was written.[6] There is, however, one source which Melville must have known at least indirectly. This is Sir Edward Davies's *The Mythology and Rites of the British Druids*. Melville read one account of Davies's works in Matthew Arnold's *On the Study of Celtic Literature* (1867), and references to them and the information they contained appeared often throughout nineteenth-century comparative mythology. According to Davies, the most important Celtic god was Hu, the "Celtic Apollo," known also as Beli and Budd.[7]

This British god was, in Davies's view, one source of the Greek gods to whom Budd is likened — Hyperion, Apollo, and Hercules. Davies claims that the Greek gods "are all plainly resolvable into one deity, *the sun*" (and, of course, are "no other than the *great patriarch*").[8] Since "the mythology of the Britons was of a character somewhat more antique than that of the Greeks and Romans . . . the Helio-Arkite god of the Britons comprehended, in his own person, most of the gods which pertained to their superstition."[9]

The god known as Hu, Beli, and Budd was seen "as the *greatest God*, and viewed as *riding on the sunbeams*, or personified in the great luminary, and operating in the clouds and meteors of heaven."[10] He is "expressly identified with Apollo, the solar divinity . . . He has also the name of *Budd, Victory*, and *Buddugre*, the '*god of victory, the king who rises in light, and ascends the sky.*'"[11]

---

[6] To gain some idea of the mass of work on the Druids, see *Druids and Druidism: A List of References,* compiled by George F. Black (New York, 1920), and the *Catalogue of the Books in the Celtic Department* of the Aberdeen University Library (Aberdeen, 1897).

[7] Davies, *Mythology,* pp. 116ff.

[8] *Ibid.,* p. 124.

[9] *Ibid.,* p. 123.

[10] *Ibid.,* p. 112.

[11] *Ibid.,* p. 116; see also *Anacalypsis,* I, 154: "they call their God Budd, the God of Victory, the king who rises in light and ascends the sky."

When Billy Budd is hanged, the ancient and modern British religions become one:

> ... the last signal, a preconcerted dumb one, was given. At the same moment it chanced that the vapory fleece hanging low in the East was shot through with a soft glory as of the fleece of the Lamb of God seen in mystical vision, and simultaneously therewith, watched by the wedged mass of upturned faces, Billy ascended; and, ascending, took the full rose of the dawn. (P. 124)

Billy Budd consistently symbolizes harmony, tranquillity, and peace, and these symbolic values are often expressed in Christian terms. The captain of the *Rights-of-Man* tells the lieutenant of the *Bellipotent*, who is about to impress Budd, that peace on the merchant ship, which only Budd has succeeded in bringing, will leave with him; and he begs him not "to take away my peacemaker!" The lieutenant's reply, an ironic rephrasing of a passage from the Sermon on the Mount, points up the central tension of *Billy Budd:* "well, blessed are the peacemakers, especially the fighting peacemakers." Just as the Sermon on the Mount supplies words to the officer whose actions mock it, Christianity itself can do no more in this man-of-war world than supply good chaplains for its men-of-war:

> Bluntly put, a chaplain is the minister of the Prince of Peace serving in the host of the God of War — Mars. As such, he is as incongruous as a musket would be on the altar at Christmas. Why, then, is he there? Because he indirectly subserves the purpose attested by the cannon; because too he lends the sanction of the religion of the meek to that which practically is the abrogation of everything but brute Force. (P. 122)

Like the modern Budd, the ancient British god was also a symbol of peace; but his peace was the peace which comes from victory. A city's civilization lies within "the established inclosure of the band of the harmonious BUDD."[12] The harmony of Budd derives from slaughter: "And this connexion between the British divinities of *slaughter* and *victory*, is marked in the character of Merdin, who is styled — *Allwedd byddin Budd Ner* — *the key, or interpreter of the army of the god of victory.*"[13] Vere speaks for Budd when he, like a dumb animal or mute god, cannot. Like Merlin (Merdin),

---

[12] Davies, *Mythology,* p. 364.
[13] *Ibid.,* p. 468.

Vere marks the connection between slaughter and harmonious victory. In the sacrifice of Billy Budd, Vere consecrates this connection, and dedicates himself and the world he commands to a harmony deriving from slaughter.

The first Handsome Sailor to appear in *Billy Budd* is worshiped like the grand sculptured bull of the Assyrian priests. The old British god Hu, Budd, or Beli — possibly the Celtic equivalent of Baal or Bel — was also often represented by a sacred bull.[14] Davies prints and twice translates a poem which describes a killing of the sacred bull, a killing which Davies says could be either an accident or a mystic ritual:

"It was my earnest wish that thou mightest live, O thou of victorious energy! Alas, thou BULL, wrongfully oppressed, thy death I deplore. Thou has been a friend of tranquility!

In view of the sea, in the front of the assembled men, and near the pit of conflict, the raven has pierced thee in wrath!"[15]

The similarities between the slaying of this sacred bull and the slaying of Billy Budd hardly need statement. Not a soul on the *Bellipotent* but earnestly wishes that Budd might live, Budd of victorious energy. Budd is indeed wrongfully oppressed, and his death is deplored by all. He has been the greatest friend of tranquillity. In view of the sea, in the front of the assembled men, and near the site of fatal conflict, Budd is ritually sacrified, sacrified because he has been pierced by the inscrutable wrath beneath Claggart's "silken jet curls."

Of course it was not for their sacrifice of bulls that the Druids were notorious. From Caesar's account on, the human sacrifices of the Druids had many chroniclers and commentators. One of the most widely known authorities was William Borlase, whose eighteenth-century research on the Druids was defended, attacked, and quoted throughout most of the nineteenth century. In a chapter entitled "Of the Druid Worship," Borlase briefly mentions that the Druids "used to sacrifice bulls" and carry "to war with them the image of a bull," but his central concern is with their human sacrifice. He points out that these sacrifices were particularly important in time of war: "For the redemption of the life of Man, they held, that nothing but the life of Man could be accepted

---

[14] *Ibid.,* p. 135.
[15] *Ibid.,* p. 577; also, slightly variant, pp. 172-73.

by the Gods; and the consequence of this was, that those who implored safety from the dangers of war . . . immediately sacrificed some human creature."[16] To secure for his world safety from the dangers of war, Captain Vere sacrifices Budd.

According to Borlase's account of the Druids' choice of sacrificial victims, Billy Budd would seem to have been an ideal selection:

> Their human sacrifice generally consisted of such criminals as were convicted of theft, or any capital crime; . . . but when such malefactors were not at hand, the innocent took their place. They held, that Man was the most precious, and therefore the most grateful victim which they could offer to their Gods; and the more dear and beloved was the person, the more acceptable they thought the offering of him would be accounted. Hence, not only beautiful captives and strangers; but Princes and the first-born of their own children, were, upon great and interesting occasions, offered upon their Altars.[17]

Billy Budd, sacrificed upon a great and interesting occasion, is a criminal convicted of a capital crime; he is innocent; he is dear and beloved by all; he is a beautiful captive; he is a stranger.

If there seem to be any contradictions between Billy Budd's role as sacrifice and his role as god, the next part of Borlase's account of Druidic sacrifice should partially resolve them:

> In order to satisfy the scrupulous of the innocence of such barbarous sacrifices, and reconcile the devoted victim to his fate, the Druids held, that the souls of those who served as victims to their Gods in this life, were deified . . . and the remains of those who died in sacrifice, were accounted most holy, and honoured before any other dead bodies.[18]

And there are other partial resolutions.

While Melville was in the early stages of composing *Billy Budd*, John Rhys published a notable work on the Celtic religions. Rhys construed the Welsh Beli to be the Irish Bili or Bile, and he translated Beli, Bili, and Bile as Death.[19] It is easy to understand what Melville meant by the name which he finally decided to give to

---

[16] *Antiquities, Historical and Monumental, of the County of Cornwall. Consisting of Several Essays on the First Inhabitants, Druid-Superstition, Customs, and Remains of the most Remote Antiquity in Britain and the British Isles* (London, 1769), pp. 126-27.
[17] *Ibid.*, p. 126.
[18] *Ibid.*

Billy Budd's ship.[20] The first half of *Bellipotent* is a complicated pun combining a Latin word for war, several of the names of Billy Budd's divine Celtic prototype, and the apparent meaning of these names; the second half suggests that this combination may triumph. Thus the name of the ship is a variant of Billy Budd's own name. For the last page of Rhys's work unites Bili with Buada, the Irish equivalent of Budd, translates these united names, and thus displays one meaning of Billy Budd and his ritual sacrifice: "Bili Buada or Bile of Victory, whose name possibly meant victorious Death."

As a sacrificial offering, Budd plays the role of both the ancient and the modern British god. Many have noticed that Christian terms and images accumulate more and more thickly around Billy Budd as he passes from sailor idol and blessed peacemaker to ritual sacrifice to sailor God. Even the change, "for special reasons," of the yardarm from which Budd is to hang accentuates his image as a Christ: instead of being hanged from the customary foreyard he is hanged from the mainyard, the yard which forms a cross with the central and highest mast.[21] But this crucifix is not merely Christian: "the cross was also used by the Druids as a sacred symbol." "The Druids seek studiously for an oak tree, large and handsome, growing up with two principal arms, *in the form of a cross*, beside the main stem, upright. If the two horizontal arms are not sufficiently adapted to the figure, they fasten a cross-beam to it."[22] Long after Budd's Christ-like and Budd-like ascension into the fleecy sky, the sailors regard the spar from which he was hanged as the true Cross:

> The spar from which the foretopman was suspended was for some few years kept trace of by the bluejackets. Their knowledges followed it from ship to dockyard and again from dockyard to ship, still pursuing it even when at last reduced to a mere dockyard boom. To them a chip of it was as a piece of the Cross. (P. 131)

---

[19] John Rhys, *Lectures on the Origin and Growth of Religion as Illustrated by Celtic Heathendom: Hibbert Lectures, 1886* (London, 1888), pp. 91, 643, 678.
[20] See pp. 20-21 of the Introduction to the Hayford-Sealts edition for the evidence that the *Bellipotent*, not the *Indomitable*, was Melville's final choice for the name of the ship.
[21] Vincent Freimarck, "Mainmast as Crucifix in *Billy Budd*," *Modern Language Notes*, LXXII (1957), 496-97.
[22] These two quotations come from E. I. Sears, "The Celtic Druids," *National Quarterly Review*, XI (1865), 1-26, a review of several eighteenth- and nineteenth-century works on the Druids, including one work by Davies and one by Godfrey Higgins. Several pages later, Sears quotes in full Borlase's account of Druidic sacrifice.

In this man-of-war world, man creates a god by hanging an idol-ized man from a warship's mainyard, and the mainyard becomes, to the commoners of this world, a true Cross to worship. The Christian terms and symbols piled upon Billy Budd thus have complicated but clearly defined functions. Obviously they exalt and extend Budd's symbolic values. The ancient British god for which Billy Budd is named certainly cannot make his ritual sacrifice as meaningful to modern readers as can the modern sacrificial god, the principal god of the Western world, the only god acknowledged by most of Melville's readers. But since Billy Budd unites the ancient and modern sacrificial gods in one body and one ritual, he embodies a comparision of the two myths. When we realize that Budd's myth is a myth consciously created by his captain, we realize that Budd also dramatizes a statement about all men's gods and shows how and why the Christian god may also have been created by man.

The mythic creation of *Billy Budd* is defined by a triangle which has for its apexes Starry Vere, Billy Budd, and Horatio Nelson. Each pair defines a line of meaning of which the third does not partake. Nelson and Budd die ritual deaths; Nelson and Vere consciously maintain the ritual around these deaths; Vere and Budd perform different parts in the same ritual. Vere does not die a ritual death; Budd is not conscious of the ritual significance; Nelson's ritual is quite different from that of Budd and Vere. Since Nelson performs the dual role of priest and sacrificial victim, his actions can be evaluated only ambiguously. Because "a sort of priestly motive" led him to adorn "*himself* for the altar and the sacrifice," his acts may be mere "vain-glory." But what if the priest were not the ritual victim, the sacrificer not the hero? What if the slayer were less willing and more knowledgeable than Nelson, and the slain as willing and less knowledgeable? These are the questions propounded by the sacrifice of Billy Budd.[23]

Unlike Nelson, Vere fights not for the glory of war but against the permanence of war. His solitary reading and thought lead him calmly to define his foe. "Captain Vere disinterestedly opposed" the revolutionary tides not alone "because they seemed to him incapable of embodiment in lasting institutions, but at war with the peace of the world and the true welfare of mankind." He seeks

---

[23] For three different treatments of Budd's death as ritual sacrifice see Tyrus Hillway, *"Billy Budd:* Melville's Human Sacrifice," *Pacific Spectator,* VI (1952), 342-47; Ray B. West, Jr., "The Unity of *Billy Budd," Hudson Review,* V (1952), 120-28; and R. H. Fogle, *"Billy Budd:* The Order of the Fall," *Nineteenth-Century Fiction,* XV (1960), 189-206.

to impose order on disorder. He interprets myth in terms of his dedication to order, and he sees that only the order dramatized by mythic ritual can prevail. Vere is the true priest of the man-of-war world which he commands and of the martial religion which orders this world.[24] With Budd's cooperation, he can maintain the rituals and myths upon which that religion depends.

Vere dissipates the last disorder of *Billy Budd* by calling for the drumbeat to quarters "at an hour prior to the customary one." "The drumbeat dissolved the multitude" because "true martial discipline long continued superinduces in average man a sort of impulse whose operation at the official word of command much resembles in its promptitude the effect of an instinct." Vere explicates the meaning of this ritual:

> "With mankind," he would say, "forms, measured forms, are everything; and that is the import couched in the story of Orpheus with his lyre spellbinding the wild denizens of the wood." And this he once applied to the disruption of forms going on across the Channel and the consequences thereof. (P. 128)

The wild denizens of Vere's wood are the men he commands, whose quick response to martial discipline is almost instinctive. Billy Budd, that tame but potent animal, is the perfect sacrifice to these measured forms. The final ritual which follows the hanging and burial of Billy Budd shows how Vere uses these forms to spellbind his wild animals:

> At this unwonted muster at quarters, all proceeded as at the regular hour. The band on the quarter-deck played a sacred air, after which the chaplain went through the customary morning service. That done, the drum beat the retreat; and toned by music and religious rites subserving the discipline and purposes of war, the men in their wonted orderly manner dispersed to the places allotted them when not at the guns. (P. 128)

---

[24] For another type of modern-day Druid, see the sketch Melville wrote at about this time and variously entitled "Asaph Blood," "Daniel Orme," and "Daniel Druid." (Hayford and Sealts correct the long-standing misimpression that this sketch was at one time part of *Billy Budd*.) It is interesting to note that Daniel Orme's counterpart on the *Bellipotent* is the Dansker, who is merely an "old Merlin" with limited oracular powers and no priestly functions. The presence of a fully developed bluejacket Druid on Vere's ship would have mitigated his priesthood of the modern Budd's religion. Vere can command at will the rituals of the "good chaplain" as he could not command a bluejacket priest.

After the demonstration of the subservience of music and religion to war and the restoration of the order in which all men are allotted places when not at their guns, comes the last paragraph of Billy Budd's story:

> And now it was full day. The fleece of low-hanging vapor had vanished, licked up by the sun that late had so glorified it. And the circumambient air in the clearness of its serenity was like smooth white marble in the polished block not yet removed from the marble-dealer's yard. (P. 128)

The ordered forms of the warship's world create a serenity symbolized by a cut and polished, but unsculptured block. This block replaces the glorious fleece.

But the end of Billy Budd's story is not the end of *Billy Budd:* "But though properly the story ends with his life, something in way of sequel will not be amiss. Three brief chapters will suffice." These three brief chapters define the ultimate significance of Vere's religion and the sacrifice of Billy Budd.

In order, they show the effect of Budd's death on the obscure death of Vere, the lies which constitute the official account of Budd's death, and the myth which the sailors make of Budd's death. After the sacrifice of Billy Budd, the *Bellipotent*, "by rare good fortune," subdues and captures "the *Athée* (the *Atheist*)." This is the symbolic triumph of a religion over atheism; the religion which triumphs is a religion of war, of death, of ancient and modern sacrificial gods. Vere, mortally wounded in this symbolic battle, gives up command and later dies ashore, murmuring "Billy Budd, Billy Budd," in what seem "not the accents of remorse." Vere, perhaps the true savior, the preserver of society, could pass to the next commander an ordered command, the ordered command which defeats the *Athée*. Thus, Vere's perservation of martial order leads to the symbolic defeat of chaos, but this chaos kills him. And his death is not the death of a Nelson or a Budd. The second chapter of the sequel quotes the only account "that hitherto has stood in human record," an account which "appeared in a naval chronicle of the time, an authorized weekly publication." This account pictures Claggart the alien serpent as the British hero and Budd the primitive British innocent as the foreign villain. Thus, not only does the martial order decree death to the destroyer of evil, but also the official understanding confuses evil and good. In the final chapter comes the bluejackets' mythical version, a version in ballad form of a truth incomprehensible to the official publication and perhaps unknown even to Vere. Vere's intellectual truth and the sailors' mythical truth enclose the official lies, and transcend, each in its way, the official order.

In *Moby-Dick* the myth created by the superstitious sailors became Ahab's myth, and he futilely tried to slay the demon of the seas of life. Billy Budd slays the serpent with inadvertent ease, and therefore man himself slays Billy Budd. An incarnate metaphysical evil destroyed Ahab. Billy Budd, immune to this evil, is destroyed by the nature of man and man's society. Vere interprets this nature and sustains the military forms which regulate and which decree Budd's death. The sailors turn these "forms, measured forms" into the ballad myth of Billy Budd. These forms and the myth which accepts them mirror a society dependent both on forms and on their mythologized statement. Myth, destructive in the worlds of *Mardi*, *Moby-Dick*, and *Pierre*, preserves the world of *Billy Budd*. Ahab destroyed all but one through a myth; Vere saves all but one through a myth. But a world in which perfect innocence must be ritually sacrificed in order to create the measured forms upon which society survives is, perhaps, quite as appalling as the world of *The Confidence-Man*.

Leonard Nathanson

"Melville's *Billy Budd*, Chapter 1"

In Chapter 1 of *Billy Budd*, Captain Graveling relates to the *Bellipotent's* lieutenant an anecdote concerning the young sailor just chosen for impressment and one Red Whiskers that is usually thought to serve the function of establishing Billy's trait of unreflective action and also of foreshadowing his killing of Claggart. The significance for the novel's plot of Billy's trashing of Red Whiskers is clear enough. "Quick as lightning Billy let fly his arm" prefigures the blow with which he strikes Claggart dead when called upon by Captain Vere to answer the Master-at-arms' accusation of intention to mutiny. "The next instant, quick as the flame from a discharged cannon at night, his right arm shot out, and Claggart dropped to the deck" (chap. 19, p. 99 in the edition by Harrison Hayford and Merton M. Sealts, Jr., Univ. of Chicago Press, 1962).

But there is also a thematic significance in the parallel of Red Whiskers and Claggart as persecutors of Billy and as "victims" of his strength. Each represents the principle of evil with which Billy

From *The Explicator,* XXII, No. 9 (May 1964). Reprinted by permission. Copyright 1964 by *The Explicator.*

comes into conflict in the two worlds of the *Rights-of-Man* and the *Bellipotent*. What is especially interesting is that both of Billy's very different antagonists are associated with the specifically infernal. It is hardly necessary to point out that Claggart is conceived along Satanic lines, since Melville has made so much explicit reference to Milton's Satan in depicting him. In his perversion of intelligence, energy, and (as is strongly hinted) noble descent into a destructive hatred that can respond only with "Pale ire, envy, and despair" to perfect innocence and perfect beauty Claggart is perhaps the most fully developed ectype of Satan to be found in modern literature. Now Red Whiskers, it should be noted, is also delineated in infernal terms. But, of course, there is no resemblance here to the Satan after whom Claggart is modeled; there is no suggestion of fallen grandeur or of perverted capacity. Red Whiskers is conceived, instead, along the lines of the popular folk devil or the "Vice." He is not the devil as suave tempter, seriously to be feared as the agent leading man to destruction, but only the half-contemptible, half-entertaining fool, easily recognized and defeated by the protagonist.

As in medieval and Renaissance popular literary tradition, the Vice is essentially a comic figure, ranging from fool to clown to ruddy devil, embodying the spirit of troublesome misrule rather than the principle of evil. It is just this absurdity that Captain Graveling recognizes when he describes Billy's opponent as the "buffer of the gang, the big shaggy chap with the fire-red whiskers." The contrast to the intelligence, elegance of person, and self-control of Claggart could hardly be sharper. Red Whiskers, as the almost emblematic color of his hair suggests, is a noisy, obtuse mischief-maker, whose belligerence earns him a drubbing, the usual punishment of the devil-as-an-ass. He is close to the absurd kind of devil to which C. S. Lewis has attempted unsuccessfully to reduce Milton's Satan, a devil, like Claggart, to whom much more is due.

Red Whiskers is the embodiment of such evil as Billy encounters in the peaceful setting of the *Rights-of-Man*, the merchant vessel so named by its "hardheaded Dundee owner [who] was a staunch admirer of Thomas Paine. . . ." When Billy leaves this ship he moves from a world of humane and liberal regard for the individual into the implacable sphere of the *Bellipotent*, where the inflexible legalism of the Mutiny Act defines innocence, guilt, and justice according "to the frontage, the appearance," as Captain Vere insists it must. In the benign world of the *Rights-of-Man*, Red Whiskers' antipathy to the beauty and innocence of Billy is overt, harmless, and comic in its outcome. Billy clears the air of all tension by giving this bully a thrashing that everyone agrees was richly deserved, including, it would seem, Red Whiskers, who surrenders his ill-feeling and is thereafter won over. While Billy can, by virtue of his physical strength and winning manner, tame and reform the devil of the *Rights-of-Man*, no such easy victory is scored in his struggle with evil aboard the *Bellipotent*. Billy's goodness and his instinctive physical response are inadequate when set against the complex and irremediable evil incarnated in Claggart, whose malice operates furtively and tenaciously to its tragic conclusion. The parallel of Red Whiskers and Claggart as antagonists of Billy is thus constructed so as to emphasize massive and ironic contrasts pertinent to the political and ethical meaning of the novel. The incident involving the comic devil looks forward to a similar yet profoundly different clash with Satan himself.

Ralph W. Willett

From "Nelson and Vere: Hero and Victim in *Billy Budd, Sailor*"

Emerson's faith in the historic role of the hero did not prevent him from evaluating Nelson morally as a man without principle.[1] Unfortunately, he failed to make his criticism specific; only the grouping of Nelson with Napoleon offers a clue to the origin of Emerson's disapproval. Hawthorne and Melville were more well-disposed in their appreciations, which resemble each other in extravagance of sentiment. Whereas Hawthorne's treatment takes the form of an essay, Melville incorporates Nelson into his short novel, *Billy Budd, Sailor,*[2] and puts to his own uses what Hawthorne called, in *Our Old Home*, the "symbolic poetry" (I, 275) of Nelson's life.

Reprinted by permission of the Modern Language Association of America from *PMLA*, LXXXII (October 1967), 370-373. Copyright 1967, by the Modern Language Association of America.
[1] *The Journals and Miscellaneous Notebooks of Ralph Waldo Emerson*, Vol. II, 1822-26, ed. William H. Gilman, Alfred R. Ferguson, Merrell R. Davis (Cambridge, Mass., 1961), p. 90.
[2] References are to the definitive edition: Herman Melville, *Billy Budd, Sailor* (*An Inside Narrative*), ed. Harrison Hayford and Merton M. Sealts, Jr. (Chicago, 1962)—hereafter cited as *Billy Budd, Sailor*. I am deeply indebted to Professor Sealts and Professor Lyon Richardson for reading this paper and offering suggestions.

Why Melville, in his last prose work, should have chosen to create a perfect hero in the figure of Nelson requires some elucidation. It is no accident that Chapters iv and v, in which Nelson appears most prominently, precede the introduction and description of Captain Vere. The historical personage and the fictional character are surely juxtaposed for the purposes of comparison. The differences between Nelson and Vere have been adequately rehearsed by various critics,[3] particularly those who see Vere as an inferior version of Nelson. The English admiral represents, for Melville, the ideal version of the governing principle; not only does Nelson help to defeat the revolutionary, anarchic ideas of the French, but he also demonstrates his ability to manage effectively any crew with traces of recalcitrance, "not indeed to terrorize the crew into bare subjection, but to win them, by force of his mere presence and heroic personality, back to . . . allegiance."[4] Vere, on the other hand, is unable to emulate this ideal; he is an illustration of Melville's contention that man, at any level below that of the hero, is the victim of his own ambiguities and inconsistencies, and of history.

The temporal context of the story is the era of the Napoleonic Wars and of the Nore Mutiny, and it is against this background that Vere's conduct has to be judged. It is the historical situation which is responsible for Vere's obsession with mutiny and which exposes his human frailty. An awareness of the possibility of mutiny at this time, a few months after the Nore incident, is, says Melville guardedly, "not unreasonable," but he also points out that such a possibility is in no way suggested by the behavior of the *Bellipotent's* crew. These circumstances, in conjunction with Claggart's machinations, Vere's temperament, and Billy's simplicity, produce the catastrophe.

Insufficient importance has been attached to Vere's irascibility, which Melville makes no attempt to hide. Normally Vere controls this instantly, but the fact remains that Claggart's accusation against Billy Budd and his frequent references to mutiny are delivered at a time when Vere is emotionally agitated. His refusal to be unduly alarmed by Claggart's "revelations" might have been sustained had his response not been followed soon afterwards by the shocking violence in his cabin. His reaction this time, excited

---

[3] See, e.g., Wendell Glick, "Expediency and Absolute Morality in *Billy Budd,*" *PMLA*, LXVIII (March 1953), 103-110, and Phil Withim, "*Billy Budd*: Testament of Resistance," *MLQ*, XX (June 1959), 115-127.

[4] *Billy Budd, Sailor*, p. 59.

and febrile, with a startling religious flavor, precludes any attempt at self-control. Billy is prejudged, as the drumhead court comes to realize (p. 108), and Vere's fears of mutiny serve to rationalize the prejudgment.

This should indicate that it is dangerous to regard Nelson and Vere as schematically arranged symbols of recklessness and prudence. Since these modes of behavior are available to both men, the difference between them narrows down to the question of the appropriate attitude for the occasion. Nelson dies glamorously, boldly, a self-sacrificing priest absolving his crew, yet he can also be circumspect, as he is when he leads the fleet up the channel to Copenhagen. Vere's background is academic and, as Melville suggests, such a training may be responsible for an ignorance of human nature. Vere is excessively cautious in discounting his intuitive knowledge of Billy Budd and Claggart,[5] and it is his generally prudent approach which, in a sense, causes his strange behavior after Billy Budd kills Claggart. Accustomed to controlling emotion as soon as it manifests itself, Vere's powers of cerebration are temporarily impaired when he is overtaken by an irresistible emotional response. Consequently, his arguments as they stand in the text are not even *a priori* reasoning, but are rationalizations of a hasty decision: "Yet the angel must hang!" (p. 101).

Vere's rashness is emphasized by Melville through two pertinent metaphors: when a ship encounters fog, "speed is put on at the hazard of running somebody down" (p. 114); the *Bellipotent's* captain is also likened to a migratory fowl which fails to notice when it crosses a frontier. But Melville's attitude toward Vere's behavior is not simply condemnatory; in Chapter xiv of *The Confidence-Man*, he argues that novelists are justified in creating inconsistent characters since life itself contains so many inconsistencies. Melville also points out in *Billy Budd, Sailor* that it is easy to be wise after the event. Irrespective of our motives, we cannot guarantee what the results of our actions will be. A superseded passage neatly illustrates this view: "the prudent method adopted by Captain Vere to obviate publicity and trouble having resulted in an event that necessitated the former, and, under existing circumstances in the navy indefinitely magnified the latter."[6] As retained passages suggest, the world is unpredictable and ironic. Violence and disorder sometimes lead to progress, as the Nore

---

[5] Vere is so impressed by Billy Budd that he thinks of promoting him; conversely he is suspicious of Claggart's "patriotism."
[6] *Billy Budd, Sailor*, p. 377, Leaf 229 c.

mutiny and the French Revolution testify; conversely, Vere's soothing words to Billy Budd have a result which is "contrary to the effect intended" (p. 99). The most clearly ironic example begins with Vere's attempt to forestall mutiny by making an example of Billy Budd; this only serves to stimulate discontent among the crew and to make Billy a martyr. And the irony is deeper yet: Vere's reputation as a seaman and fighter is, among the officers, as high as Nelson's, yet it is through Vere that Billy Budd joins Nelson in the realm of naval myth and naval hagiology, a more enduring sort of fame.

Only the responsible hero can be relied upon to impose harmony and to neutralize the effects of chance, and a clearer idea of Melville's conception of a great man can be obtained by an examination of Carlyle's *Lectures on Heroes, Hero-Worship and the Heroic in History* (1841-46). This work, when drawn into critical service, illuminates both Lord Nelson and, to a lesser extent, Captain Vere, for these figures grow in solidity as the resemblances between Carlyle's theory and Melville's fictional actuality are observed.

In Carlyle's dogmatic eulogies we find the conception of the hero which was to inform Melville's book in the shape of Lord Nelson. What is almost Carlyle's first observation brings Nelson and the British Navy to mind: "We cannot look, however imperfectly, upon a great man, without gaining something by him. He is the living light-fountain, which is good and pleasing to be near."[7] This surely is Melville's view of Nelson, a glowing figure in "the jewelled vouchers of his own shining deeds" (p. 58), inspiring his men at Trafalgar and elsewhere. (The definition of character in terms of light also occurs in *The Confidence-Man,* where the original character is described as being "like a revolving Drummond light, raying away from itself all around it — everything is lit by it, everything starts from it.")[8] Moreover, Nelson seeks and achieves a hero's end: "Difficulty, abnegation, martyrdom, death" (p. 64) — these, says Carlyle, are allurements to the heart of the heroic man. Thus it is with Nelson, "a reckless declarer of his person in fight," unafraid to face death and to become a martyr.

Yet Melville, like Carlyle, does not consider the hero merely in abstract conceptual terms; for both writers, great men form part of their interpretation of history and of their political ideologies.

---

[7] Thomas Carlyle, *Lectures on Heroes, Hero-Worship and the Heroic in History,* ed. P. C. Parr (Oxford, 1925), p. 1.

[8] Herman Melville, *The Confidence-Man: His Masquerade* (New York, 1961), p. 278.

Carlyle indicates the decay and ruin that result from rebellion but at the same time optimistically points to the hero as "the one fixed point in revolutionary history," a cornerstone standing firm amidst the maelstrom of social chaos. For Melville also, the hero represented by Nelson is a stabilizing figure, well equipped to suppress and control insurrections. As Melville's story reveals, Nelson was transferred to the *Theseus,* a ship which had taken part in the Nore mutiny, in order to win over the crew by means of his magnetic personality. The occasion, it seems, calls forth the man whether it be one of Carlyle's heroes, Cromwell, at the time of the English Civil War, or Melville's Nelson at the time of the Napoleonic wars.

However, these heroes are not just examples of historical con-catenations. What the hero is and what he does are morally and socially desirable. Carlyle is able to affirm that "society is founded on hero-worship" (p. 11), and his reasons are not difficult to find: "every Great Man . . . is by the nature of him a son of Order, not of Disorder. . . . He is the missionary of Order. Is not all work of man in this world a *making of order?*" (p. 185). Thus he articulates the ideas which concerned Melville increasingly during the latter part of his life.

Nelson, who emerges as a result of Melville's lifelong concern with order, fits neatly into Carlyle's last category, the hero as King, that is, "the Commander over men." This type of hero, in Carlyle's view, is "practically the summary for us of *all* the various figures of Heroism; Priest, Teacher . . . to *command* over us . . . to tell us for the day and hour what we are to *do*" (p. 178). Carlyle had earlier referred to "the wayfaring and battling priest," and Melville explicitly sees Nelson in these terms, a man of "priestly motive" and one of the moving forces in the "plenary absolution" the English sailors received through the battle of Trafalgar. (By this token, Billy Budd, too, has traces of the heroic, for he is a "fighting peacemaker" and is compared to a Catholic priest.)

Yet it is not only the positive qualities of men in high positions which find their way from Carlyle's pages to Melville's. "A man is right and invincible, virtuous . . . when he joins himself to the great deep Law of the World, in spite of all superficial laws, temporary appearances, profit-and-loss calculations" (p. 51), says Carlyle, and the violation of this precept is clearly enacted by Captain Vere, who chooses to embrace man-made laws and to reject God's law: "At the Last Assizes it [the officer of marines' plea] shall acquit. But how here? We proceed under the law of the Mutiny Act."[9]

In other ways, too, Vere is the negation of Carlyle's and Melville's "Great Man." He lacks the spontaneity that characterizes Carlyle's hero, being rather a man of prudence, the naval counterpart of the Benthamite utilitarians who evoke the scorn of both writers. In addition, he is, unlike the hero, a creature of his time, a captain whose emotional balance and patterns of thought are dictated by historical pressures.

Amidst the correspondences of accepted values, one sharp difference stands out. Carlyle is heartened by his great men in the very process of describing them and their abilities. His treatment of revolutions and disintegration, though relevant, is brief, and he looks forward to an Emersonian world in which every man achieves his own kind of greatness. For Melville, on the other hand, the hero is a rarity, a kind of biological sport; much more common is the imperfect leader or unheroic administrator. Vere partakes of the work of man as defined by Carlyle, but cannot impose order through the exhibition of a heroic personality. This is his tragedy and by implication the world's.

The interesting parallels between Carlyle's and Melville's ideas of the hero-type are but one kind of evidence, and the importance of that evidence would be negligible were it not buttressed by similar indications in the text itself. Consequently, an examination of the stages of development in the novella, and of Melville's revisions, is not without relevance to the Nelson-Vere relationship.

Chapters iii to v in *Billy Budd, Sailor*, which are the chief 'Nelson' sections, reveal a figure who fulfils two roles, those of peacemaker and of reckless hero. Both these functions are put in the narrative at an early stage (Bb),[10] but whereas the transfer in Chapter v of Nelson to a ship with an intractable crew receives no later addition or elaboration, Nelson's foolhardy heroism in Chapter iv is later augmented at stage G during the period when Melville decided tentatively to restore that chapter. His hesitancy over the inclusion of Chapter iv, which was only reintroduced during the post-D stage, and even then was kept in a separate folder, should not lead the reader to doubt the author's intention, since there remains sufficient material to link Nelson and Vere. Indeed, the fact that the Nelson chapter (iv) and one of the Vere

---

[9] *Billy Budd, Sailor*, p. 111.
[10] For a full description of the stages, see the definitive edition, *Billy Budd, Sailor*, pp. 236-239.

chapters (vii) were kept separately would seem to indicate that they were connected in Melville's scheme. Moreover, we have Hayford's evidence that Melville revised the scene between Vere and the surgeon shortly after revising the Nelson chapter: he used the verso of superseded Bb leaf 16[5] for the new leaf 41 (post-G pencil), in the revised Vere-surgeon scene.[11]

The restoration stage comes after the extensive additions to the characterization of Vere in Chapters vi and vii, and the sharpening of the contrast between "martial glory" and prudence in Chapter iv obviously refers to Vere's undemonstrative appearance and his avoidance of injudiciously intrepid behavior. Melville leaves no doubt when, in the final pencil stage, Vere's lack of brilliancy is emphasized.

Whereas both Billy Budd and Nelson are presented as peacemakers at stage Bb, the development of Vere in this role proceeds piecemeal during the later stages. At E, his concern for the men's welfare is made part of the narrative, and at F his ideas of peace and, more especially, discipline are stated. It is at this stage too, however, that Melville begins to show how limited is Vere's success in keeping the peace, a result further emphasized at stage G. Three times ominous murmurs emanate from the crew, accompanied on one occasion by a restless movement. The crew is still governed by rigid discipline, but ironically there is more real need for strictness now. Indeed, Vere's knowledge of and the men's adherence to usage, and references by both Vere and Melville to the crew's unquestioning obedience (pp. 87, 112, 127), show how ill-founded is one, at least, of Vere's reasons for executing Billy Budd. But the chief additions at stage G both clarify Vere's dilemma sympathetically and criticize his actions (insofar as the other officers are sceptical). Thus Melville increases the ambiguity and attempts to preclude a simplistic view of Vere as a melodramatic villain.

Revisions of the text by Melville substantiate the interpretation already outlined. Wrestling with language in an attempt to convey his horror of disorder, Melville found his needed tool in the word "mutiny." Not only is it frequently used in original drafts, but "two outbreaks" become "the two mutinies," and "naval insurrection" is changed to "the Great Mutiny" (pp. 307-308). (In a pencil revision, Nelson, a queller of mutiny, is capitalized as "the Great Sailor" somewhat earlier in the text.) Melville's fondness for the word is not unrelated to his characterization of Captain Vere, who

---

[11] *Ibid.*, p. 246.

uses the Mutiny Act as justification when he advocates the execution of Billy Budd. In a superseded passage he affirms that "the blow itself, setting aside its consequence, was mutiny" and as such was "a capital crime" (p. 391). All this was true under Article XXII of the Articles of War; Billy Budd was indictable and punishable by death for striking a superior officer during time of war.[12] It is strange then that Vere should refer continually to the Mutiny Act, which was a military, not a naval statute, but his confusion can be understood in the light of his excessive fear of mutiny, and as a projection of Melville's own sentiments. Moreover, the change in the text which Melville makes on page 396 ("Mutiny Act" becomes "Articles of War") suggests Melville was hoping to convey the confusion and agitation Vere was experiencing.

Although Melville describes and comments on Vere's actions and their consequences in such a way that they cannot be evaluated superficially, he did augment the criticism levelled at Vere in late stages and revisions. These shifts of perspective are worth noting, but they should be related to the full and ambiguous context. What can at least be affirmed is that Melville's revisions do prevent the reader from seeing Vere as another Nelson.

The captain is originally described as "a sailor of distinction even in a time prolific of naval heroes," but Vere is no hero, so "naval heroes" is reduced to "renowned seamen" (p. 309). Moreover, the comparison with Peter the Barbarian, implementing criticism of Vere's secrecy, originally read "Peter the Great, chiefly Great by his crimes" (p. 384). This was softened and the irony of Vere's "barbarism," seen in contrast to Billy Budd's innocent barbarism, is artistically more satisfying, though the previous harshness does show the direction Melville's thoughts were taking at that stage (Ga). It was at the same stage that Melville introduced the discussion of sanity and insanity, after the surgeon questions Vere's mental condition, and it is significant that Melville's final comments on Claggart (in the late pencil stage) concentrate on lunacy, at a time, of course, when Vere was very much in his mind. The references on pages 336-337 to secrecy, to the seeming rationality of insane actions and to the occasional nature of such actions (for they are "evoked by some special object") would not be out of place in the passage after the Vere-surgeon scene.

Significant revisions of the characterization of Nelson are few, but, as one would expect, they tend to increase his stature. The

---

[12] See John McArthur, *Principles and Practice of Naval and Military Courts Martial,* 4th ed., 2 vols. (London, 1813), I, 333.

fleet becomes his fleet, and Trafalgar becomes great not merely in
"naval annals" but also in "human annals" (p. 302). (Also the
phrase "unique hero" was considered before "the Great Sailor" was
restored — p. 305.) Of greater importance is Melville's pencilled
notation at the bottom of Leaf 61 (p. 304): "XX the mark on the
deck where he fell." In the next leaf, the mark becomes a star, but
Melville's term of reference here is metaphorical since the mark
is in fact a silver plate.[13] Melville, in using the word "star," would
seem to be indicating ironically the connection between Nelson and
"Starry Vere," who lacked any brilliant qualities.

---

[13] See Herman Melville, *Moby-Dick* (New York, 1950), p. 39.